UNDERSTANDING THE GOLF SWING

Manuel de la Torre

UNDERSTANDING THE GOLF SWING

Warde Publishers, Inc.

Portola Valley, California

Warde Publishers, Inc.
3000 Alpine Road
Portola Valley, CA 94028
(800) 699-2733

de la Torre, Manuel, 1921–
    Understanding the golf swing / Manuel de la Torre.—
1st. ed.
    p.   cm.
    Includes index.
    ISBN: 1-886346-51-8
    1. Swing (Golf)   I. Title.
GV979.S9D45 2001   796.352′3
                     QBI01-200368

FIRST EDITION
Printed in the United States of America
10 9 8 7 6 5 4 3   04 03 02 01

Warde Publishers, Inc. and the author disclaim responsibility for adverse effects or consequences from the misapplication or injudicious use of the information contained in this book. Mention of resources and associations does not imply endorsement by Warde Publishers, Inc., or the author.

Jacket and text design by Detta Penna
Production and composition by Penna Design and Production
Photography by Luis de la Torre, Hinsdale Studio

Dedication

I dedicate this book to the memory of my father, Angel de la Torre,
the first Spanish golf professional and the person to whom
I owe my success in the golf profession. His knowledge of the golf swing
and his ability to teach it remain unequaled to this day.

He and I had a marvelous relationship, not only as father and son but in golf instruction as well. He was an excellent player in his day, having won the Spanish Open six times. His knowledge of tournament attitudes and techniques have been invaluable to me as a competitor.

Anytime he or I thought of a new teaching technique or a new way of applying our teaching principles, there would be hours of discussion and hours spent on the golf course trying out the new way or new approach to determine the validity of the new idea before trying it out on our students. Sometimes we proved that what seemed a better way was not a better way at all, and was far from being successful. Sometimes to our delight what we tried did prove to be a better way.

I admired my father for teaching me so many things about the golf swing, but especially his conviction that when a student was told to do something, the more the student did it the better the results were to be. Nothing should be told to a student that could be overdone, because if it were overdone, it would create another problem that would have to be corrected in the future. He taught me so many things, not only about golf, but about people and about life. I am most grateful to him for all of that.

Not only was Angel de la Torre exceptional in the golf profession, he was an exceptional human being, and he was exceptional in his relationships with people. All who knew him never forgot him and never an unkind word was said about him.

Contents

Part III Cause and Effect and Corrections

Part IV Special Shots

Foreword

by Carol Mann

I was inducted into the LPGA Hall of Fame in 1977, the Women's Sports Foundation Hall of Fame in 1983, and The World Golf Hall of Fame in 1998. Between July 1962 and 1977 I received an astounding education in golf—the golf swing, appropriate goal setting, and how to compete—from Manuel de la Torre. His instruction made it possible for me to pursue my passion for playing golf at the highest level even under the most intense pressure.

I joined the LPGA Tour as a somewhat ragged rookie in 1961, with no idea how to play the kind of golf that wins championships. One of the best players in the world then was Mickey Wright, winner of 82 tournaments, whose golf swing Ben Hogan called "the best of all time, man or woman." Then, as now, the older, more veteran players of the Tour often helped younger struggling ones. Mickey Wright became one of my friends and she suggested I read Ernest Jones' book *Swing the Clubhead,* during the summer of my rookie year. I read this book and was fascinated by its simple concept.

During the winter of 1962 in Dunedin, Florida I told a club professional friend, Mike Cavanaugh, what I had discovered in Jones' book. Mike turned to me and said, "I work for a pro who teaches Jones' principles. How would you like to come see him in Milwaukee?" Excited, but skeptical about my chances, sheepishly I asked, "Could I? Do you think he would see me? When?" Mike assured me that he could arrange it. The Tour had a stop in Milwaukee later that summer, so I waited until then, little knowing that this occasion would change my future.

Manuel was the head professional at the Milwaukee Country Club. His lesson tee was a private area set on an outcropping of the hillside to the left and below the first tee. I'll never forget walking down the tree-lined, shadowy, narrow footpath, with Mike leading the way. I was nervous and excited.

Manuel is a striking man, thick-chested, with handsome features, wearing rimless eyeglasses (ahead of his time!). He was very pleasant and gracious, greeting me with a smile and a strong warm handshake. After a few warm-up shots he asked, "What are you trying to do?" I fell right into his trap by reciting the litany of things I was working on during the past year or so. There were probably eight specific positions or actions I was trying to produce. Of course, I already knew it was not possible to do all of them at once. My overall method of achieving flush contact with great power was in pieces. There was no glue connecting everything together.

Manuel coaxed and coerced with his questions, enabling me to see that I was really only trying to produce one thing—a swing! I left that first session feeling as if I had discovered the Holy Grail. Everything Manuel said made so much sense.

My energy and motivation, already high, increased dramatically. I could not wait to play in the pro-am part of the tournament the next day. I started making notes immediately and wrote for a couple more hours that night. Manuel didn't know it but he had created a monster when he took me on as a student. I became a sponge for learning from him. Our sessions might end at dark and then continue in the golf shop for hours more—questioning and answering, looking at the films of my swing, discussing great players' swings, or reviewing current magazine articles. I was at a "Golf University" when I was with Manuel. I went to the local college bookstore and found two books: one on the brain, including motor learning, and the second, *Physics Without Math*, on explanations of objects in motion, actions and reactions, etc. I felt my intellectual heavens had parted because of Manuel's knowledge, patience, and extraordinarily selfless willingness to help me learn. No one ever had a better teacher for any subject.

First of all, Manuel taught me a simpler approach to the swing. He also taught me the ball flights that are essential for any tournament player—to be able to shape shots and alter trajectories. His perspective of cause and effect was the soundest basis for problem solving on or off the course that I have ever heard. I learned an array of shots, some of which today's players still do not know.

Probably the most important of Manuel's teachings was how to use my mind to direct my physical actions. It seems our notion—if we are performing a sport—is to work with the body only. How can we make ourselves understand that the mind directs the body to do what we want the body to do?

I worked on my mental discipline as often as I hit golf balls, ultimately developing it into perhaps my most useful tool during competition. Instead of focusing on all that could go wrong and what the outcomes might be, Manuel taught me to think completely, but simply and "in the present" concerning what I wanted to do. I can testify that learning to think like this prepares the mind for action even under the greatest of pressures. But you *must* know what you want to do. Oh my, I sound like Manuel! Unfortunately too many of us do not know what we want to do, or what we want to do is incorrect, or we overload our minds with too many things to do.

Manuel is a patient, kind man who cares passionately that you learn to play golf with greater ease and success. I'll never forget the period when my ball striking became much better but my scores didn't reflect the improvement due to poor putting. I became extremely agitated, impatient, and frustrated so I went to Milwaukee with an emotional edge. Fear and doubt, which are the absolute worst feelings for a driven tournament player, clouded my putting performance. They would certainly thwart a career.

At my 6:30 appointed time, Manuel entered the putting green circle in front of the clubhouse, happy, smiling, walking briskly, and eager to work. I started complaining. My attitude was pitiful. He asked again, "What are you trying to do?" Of course, I was trying to "make these putts so I can score lower!" Manuel proposed that I was misplacing my focus and attention by trying to create the outcome of making putts. He suggested that I "roll the ball, on the line you select, as far as the hole." Pretty soon I started yelling that this idea could not possibly work because I *had to try to make the putt.* Imagine—I was yelling at my teacher on his home ground!

Manuel, I say again, was as patient as a saint with me. He didn't raise his voice or change his attitude one iota for one second. Thank heavens I had the good sense to trust him. Eventually I did adopt Manuel's concept of rolling the ball . . . and went on to use it to win 37 LPGA titles and the U.S. Women's Open. I set scoring records repeatedly. At one point I even won *Golf Magazine's* "Putter of the Year" by a vote of my peers. I became a very good putter.

Letting go of my old notions of the swing and putting was a process of transformation. Manuel provided stability and constancy with his beliefs. His thorough comprehension of the swing, and the blend of mental and physical skills needed for performing it, allows me to say that he is by far the best teacher I have ever had or have knowledge of.

I am so glad for Manuel and for you that he dedicated years to writing this book. The results of his lifelong study, learning, and teaching deserve to be shared with everyone.

You will decide how he can help you. Be prepared to read this book more than once. Be prepared to think about many of Manuel's profoundly simple ideas. Be prepared to abandon some long-held myths. Be prepared to have others disagree with you. Be prepared to hear, "It can't be that easy!" Be prepared to use your mind to direct your golf actions. Be prepared to become more aware during the swing. Tune in. You will be amazed to discover your sensitivity to it. Be prepared to discard chaos while practicing or on the course. Be prepared to be less emotional. Be prepared to commit to a new way of being on the course. Be prepared to enjoy learning and playing in a full, rich state, blending mind, body, and club.

After you read this book and if you assimilate and follow Manuel's teaching, you will join me in thanking Manuel de la Torre every day of your golfing life.

Carol Mann
The Woodlands, Texas

Introduction

My only golf teacher, since the time I was two years old, has been my father, Angel de la Torre. He made tiny golf clubs for me and I began swinging those clubs and hitting balls long before I could speak. This alone says something about the golf swing and the basic simplicity and naturalness that are involved—a naturalness and simplicity, however, that incorrect priorities and incorrect thinking destroy. This book represents my views developed over the many years I have been playing and teaching golf. I have been guided by the appreciation of the truth and value in the views of Ernest Jones and my father, to which I have given my own interpretation.

Angel de la Torre

Angel and Manuel de la Torre

1

Several years before I was born, shortly after World War I, my father had met Ernest Jones, an English golf professional, while playing tournaments in Europe. Ernest Jones had been wounded during the war and as a consequence had lost his right leg. Perhaps this injury made it necessary for him, already a dedicated golf professional, to search for what really was of basic importance in the golf swing. In any case, he arrived at a concept that was very new, very different, and in many ways revolutionary in the teaching of golf. Ernest Jones and my father shared a passion for the game and, as they became lifelong associates and friends, their teachings eventually merged into a single philosophy.

When both families eventually settled in this country, the de la Torre and the Joneses spent many evenings together and their discussions, along with my very early experience in Spain, shaped my attitude toward golf and the golf swing: The golf swing is a simple and natural movement. It should be as easy to understand and teach as it was to produce.

These sessions were indeed exciting—listening to two very enthusiastic professionals tear the golf swing apart and then put it back together again. From listening I came to understand Ernest Jones' ideas, and this understanding made my father's instruction in subsequent years a great deal easier, because I understood what he was asking me to do.

Everything seemed so simple, so basically sound, and so easily understood. As I grew older I kept asking myself why so few professionals taught Ernest Jones' principles. To this day I cannot understand why. In contrast, I have been intrigued by the many theories regularly being advanced for propelling the golf ball. Some of these are so complicated that it is a wonder to me that those who propose them really feel they can be taught, let alone learned by any individual. *The Ernest Jones view is a holistic view of the movement and it coincides with the physics of motion, velocity, and force. A great difference is that the Jones concept deals with the movement of the club in concert with these basic principles and not with the movement of the body and its positions so important in the teachings of others.*

The point here is twofold. Recall the slings of early historic times, which evolved as the most simple, energy-efficient way for an individual to propel a heavy weight a long distance merely by swinging that weight in a circular motion and then releasing one arm of the sling. In tropical countries you still see this method used to hurl a heavy rock with enough force and accuracy to bring down a coconut from a tall coconut palm.

Swinging is the most energy efficient method of producing the force necessary to hurl an object a great distance.

The first point here is that a true swinging motion must be made, a movement necessarily devoid of energy-robbing leverage. In golf, the club is not released to fly off in the distance but instead its energy is transferred to the golf ball on impact and *it* flies off to its destination. However, the physics principles involved are similar.

Secondly, does anyone think that these "swingers" learned to perform these feats by trying to imitate the positions of others? Was David thinking of how his left arm should be when he used his sling against Goliath? Think of how you produce your signature. Is your attention on the movement of the hand and arm, or is it on your mental picture of what you want to produce?

In golf, the golf club is the tool that by its motion propels the golf ball. Of course your body has to move, for it is connected to the club by the hands and arms. But, is this where your attention should be directed? Is this where your attention is when you sign your name? How successful do you think you would be in teaching someone to duplicate your signature by telling that person *how* or *how much* their hand and arm should move? In golf it is no different—those questions of *how* or *how much* have no practical answers and thus are the wrong questions to ask.

As Ernest Jones, my father, and I have viewed this: *The function of the body is simply to respond to the movement we are producing with the club. If the body is allowed to be truly responsive, the movement of the body and the club will be compatible and correct.*

When I have a new student, I always ask "what are you trying to do?" and invariably the answer is one or several of the following: "I am trying to keep my head down, I am trying to keep my left arm straight, I am trying to keep my right elbow close to my body, I am trying to follow through, I am trying to finish with my hands high, I don't want to be flat, etc., etc., etc." Notice that in this entire list the golf club has not been mentioned.

Quite a few years ago I had a student who gave me these same answers, and when the list was complete I asked that the club be given back to me. I teed up a ball and asked the student to send it to a particular target. I received a suspicious look and was asked for a club. Then I said, "do you realize the number of things you told me you have to do to hit the golf ball? You never mentioned the golf club, so I assumed you did not need one." This student suddenly realized the truth—*the club cannot be ignored.*

Surrender to the importance of the club and its movement detailed in the chapters that follow. I can assure you, you will find a much more meaningful approach toward playing a game that is unequaled in the satisfaction that can be derived from playing it well.

I mentioned that I have added my own interpretations to Ernest Jones' methods. I would like to be more specific.

Ernest Jones states that you swing the clubhead with the hands but makes no distinction between the backswing and forward swing. I feel that there is a great difference. I strongly believe that in the backswing, the clubhead should be swung back with the hands, and I believe just as strongly that the clubhead should be swung forward but not with the hands. What then must be used to swing the clubhead in the forward swing? The answer is **the arms**.

I have found that when I tell a student that I would like to have him swing the clubhead with the hands on the forward swing, that the student will invariably throw the clubhead at the ball as he produces the forward swing.

By changing the words "swing the clubhead with the hands" on the forward swing to **"swing the entire club (not just the clubhead) with the arms from the end of the backswing to the finish of the swing,"** there is a tremendous difference in the way a student reacts to the instruction. Basically, all I have changed is words to give students a different mental picture of the correct motion and the result is that indeed the clubhead is truly swung. The Ernest Jones concept has remained intact.

Acknowledgments

I would like to thank all the PGA and LPGA professionals who were trusting enough to allow me to help them with their golf swings and their golf games. With some I only worked once or twice but with others the partnership lasted a number of years. They supplied me with a tremendous number of thrills as they succeeded in their goals and became winners. It is a great feeling having been involved in their success. For that, I will be forever grateful. They are Tommy Aaron, Pam Barnett, Bob Brue, Mary Lou Crocker, Betty Ferguson, Pam Higgins, Carol Mann, Mary Mills, Martha Nause, Candy Phillips, Sherri Steinhauer, Sandra Spuzich, and Peggy Wilson. I am most thankful to the Milwaukee Country Club Board of Directors for granting permission to have the photographs for this book taken at their fine golf course. I also wish to express my most sincere gratitude to my brother, Luis de la Torre, who spent a great deal of time helping me to get this book ready for publication. He is responsible for all the photographic work.

In search of better golf,

Manuel de la Torre

A Note to the Reader

This book has been divided into various sections covering different aspects of the game. Some help you to build your swing, some teach you what to do to play different types of shots while others offer you different ways to correct your swing. It suits the purpose of all types of players as well as golf instructors.

How to Use This Book

If you are a beginner, you should concentrate on Parts I and II. When you start improving, you should proceed to sections 7 and 8 in Part IV.

If you are an established player, every section of the book will be helpful with special emphasis on section 9 in Part IV, and all sections in Part V.

Regardless of your playing ability, if a certain part of your game seems to present some difficulty you should refer to that section which discusses that part of your game.

- If you are having problems with ball flight patterns, refer to Part III.

- If your problem is sand play, refer to Part IV, section 6.

- If your problem is chipping or pitching, refer to Part IV, section 7.

- If your problem is putting, refer to Part IV, section 8.

- If you wish to add versatility to your game, refer to part IV, section 9.

- If your problem is performing on the golf course, refer to Part V, sections 11, 12, 13, and 14.

The Swing

If you look up the word *swing* in the dictionary, it is defined as a backward and forward movement or a to-and-fro movement.

Being a movement, the golf swing should be studied, produced, and felt as a movement.

It is the movement of the golf club as a whole that we should be concerned with.

The swinging motion of the golf club is not a series of actions or parts which, even if they could be learned, can be put together consciously to achieve a single smooth movement. If the swinging motion were attempted as a series of actions, then after one action has been completed, something else would have to be done to produce the next one, failing to produce the smoothness and the continuity that the golf swing must have.

The emphasis in this interpretation of the golf swing is on the *golf club*. It is the tool we must *use properly* in order to send the golf ball to a specific target, while allowing everything else that happens to be a direct result of the club's motion—*the swing*.

The most enjoyable thing about this way of interpreting and producing the golf swing is the few things that you have to keep in mind or think about while executing a golf shot. Since it only takes about 2.5 seconds to make a golf swing, one cannot expect to think about more than one thing in such a short time span. Players who try to think of four, five, or more things invariably forget all but one. In the next shot, they will think of one of the forgotten ones, but still forget the rest.

In my opinion, this is the proper approach to the golf swing. You do not have to think about keeping your left arm straight, keeping your head down, consciously shifting your weight on the forward swing, keeping your elbow close to your body, pulling down with your left hand to start the forward swing, snapping your wrists to generate power as the club nears the ball, etc.

The swinging concept maintains that if you produce a swinging motion with the golf club:

1. The left arm *will* be extended (not straight) by the centrifugal force produced by the swinging motion. It simply has to be responsive.

2. The head *will* remain down sufficiently long through the instinctive human reaction of looking at whatever is going to be struck.

3. The weight *will* transfer to the left foot (right foot for left-handed players) after the club strikes the ball by having the body *respond* to the centrifugal force created by the swinging motion.

4. The body turn that takes place on the forward swing as the body responds to the club's swinging motion *will* produce a definite closeness of the body and the right elbow. *It is not the elbow that gets close to the body.*

5. By using the arms in the forward swing, the club *will* start correctly from the beginning of the forward swing without trying to use a pulling action with the left hand (right hand for left-handed players) to start it.

6. Wrist action *will* be an involuntary reaction to the coiling action (backswing) and the uncoiling action (forward swing) of the club. It is caused by the circular motion needed to swing the club over the right shoulder (left shoulder for left handed players). In the forward swing it is caused by the centrifugal force created through the swinging motion.

The problem with trying to do any of these things consciously is that we overdo them, and, furthermore, whatever we try to do will be at the wrong time.

To repeat, the emphasis in our presentation is that, having set the club on a true swinging motion the golfer must then allow the body to respond to the motion of the swing itself.

In Chapter 4 we discuss how to develop a true swinging motion with the golf club. First though it is important to understand that proper grip, stance, and alignment are essential preparations to a consistent swing.

Part I

Preparing to Swing: Grip, Stance, and Alignment

Chapter 1

The Grip

The golf club is an implement, a tool we hold in our hands to propel a golf ball in a certain direction, and the way it is held is extremely important. There are various ways of positioning the hands on the club, but they should be placed in such a way that it is easy for the player to return the clubhead to the ball so that it is at a right angle to the line in which the golf ball is to be sent.

Note: If you are a left handed golfer you have to reverse the reaction of the hand positions.

The Overlapping Grip

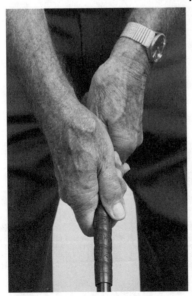

Figure 1

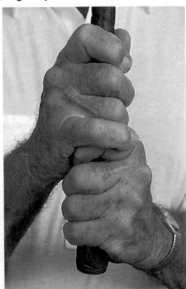

Figure 2

- For right-handed players, the high hand is the left hand, the low hand is the right hand.

- For left-handed players, the high hand is the right hand, the low hand is the left hand.

Three types of grips are in common use, and their names describe each one.

Overlapping Grip: The little finger of the low hand is placed over the index finger of the high hand. See Figures 1 and 2.

Interlocking Grip: The little finger of the low hand interlocks with the index finger of the high hand. See Figures 3 and 4.

Ten Finger Grip: All ten fingers are in contact with the club. This is commonly known as the baseball grip. See Figures 5 and 6.

Before considering these grips in detail, you should understand some very important characteristics that all the grips have in common.

The Interlocking Grip

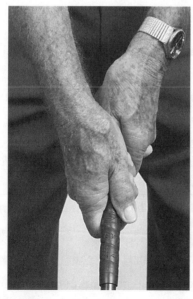
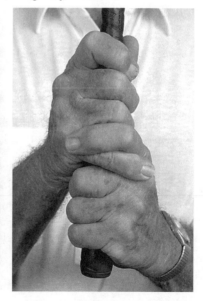

Figure 3	*Figure 4*

The Ten Finger Grip

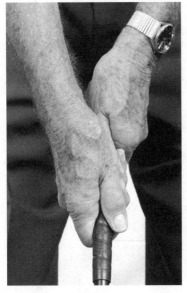
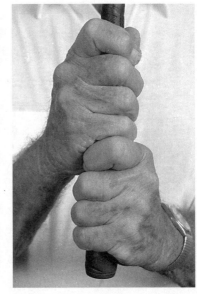

Figure 5   Figure 6

1. The club rests diagonally across the palm of the high hand. If the club is placed too far toward the fingertips, when the holding pressure is applied, the club will be rotated by the fingers and the clubhead will end up closed.

2. The club rests diagonally across the fingers of the low hand in the overlapping and interlocking grips. In the ten finger grip, the club also rests diagonally across the palm of the low hand.

3. The **V** formed by the thumb and index finger of each hand should point to the center of the body.

    What can be expected if the **V**s are not lined up to the center of the body?

    a. **V** of high hand centered and **V** of low hand points to right shoulder: At time of contact with the ball, the clubhead will be closed.

    b. **V** of low hand centered and **V** of high hand points to right shoulder: At time of contact with the ball, the clubhead will be closed.

c. **V** of high hand points to left shoulder and **V** of low hand centered: At time of contact with the ball, the clubhead will be open.

d. **V** of low hand points to left shoulder and **V** of high hand centered: At time of contact with the ball, the clubhead will be open.

e. **V** of both hands point toward the right shoulder: The clubhead will be closed at time of contact with the ball, but the effect will be double that of a and b.

f. **V** of both hands point toward the left shoulder: The clubhead will be open at time of contact with the ball, but the effect will be double that of c and d.

g. **V** of each hand point in opposite directions (one toward the left shoulder and one toward the right shoulder): Most unpredictable since it is very difficult to have both hands working in the same direction, therefore, whichever hand becomes dominant during the swing will affect the clubhead at the moment of ball contact.

4. When the hands are opened:

a. The palms should face each other.

b. The fingers will point vertically downward.

With the hands in the position described, *they are in balance*:

- With each other
- With the clubhead
- With the target line—the direction in which the ball is to be sent

When the hands are in balance, they do not work against each other, they always complement each other.

When the grip is properly taken, if you open your hands, the palm of your low hand should be facing a direction parallel to the target line. See Figure 7. The face of the clubhead will then also be at a right angle to that target line at the moment of impact.

If you use your hand to hit the ball such as when playing handball, the palm of the hand making contact with the ball will be facing the direction in which the ball is to be sent. In golf, since we are using two hands, if the palm of the low hand is facing a line parallel to the target line, the high hand will be facing the opposite direction. Thus the hands will be in a palm to palm relationship.

It is not difficult to have a good grip, if the reasons for it are understood and accepted.

Target line

Figure 7

When there is a defect in the grip, in order to have the clubhead meet the ball so that it is at a right angle to the target line, the player has to make some sort of compensating action or movement to send the ball straight to the target. The problem with this compensation is that it has to be exactly the right amount every time the club is swung. If it is more or less than needed, accuracy will not be very good. When the grip is correct, there is no need for these compensating actions or movements.

Overlapping Grip

In the overlapping grip, the high hand is placed on the club first and usually it is placed correctly without much difficulty. Fitting the low hand with the high hand is another matter—the problem is usually the little finger of the low hand. It is responsible, most of the time, for the incorrect positioning of the low hand. Most golfers think that in order to feel that their grip is secure and powerful, the little finger must be hooked around so that it reaches the knuckles of the high hand. This is a false interpretation of security and power, even though it may be real in the player's mind.

16

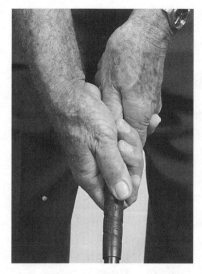

Figure 8

The little finger is quite short and to reach the knuckles of the high hand, it forces the low hand to slide under the shaft so that the palm is almost facing the sky. See Figure 8. In this position, the low hand will influence the clubhead to be very closed. Getting the golf ball into the air will be difficult, and if it does rise, it will curve rapidly to the left for right-handed players and to the right for left-handed players. The little finger of the low hand should be the last finger to be placed, not the first. Place the hands correctly on the club without the little finger, and then let the little finger fold naturally over the index finger of the high hand. This will eliminate the problem completely.

Interlocking Grip

The interlocking grip is taken by placing the high hand on the club in the same manner as in the overlapping grip, but when the low hand is placed on the club the little finger is interlocked with the index finger of the high hand. The thumb of the high hand may remain in the same position as in the overlapping grip, inside the low hand, or it may be placed over the fingers of the high hand, outside of the low hand.

This hand position has the disadvantage of separating the thumb and index finger of the high hand, a most important combination for control and feel in both hands. However, for those who wish to use the interlocking grip, be sure that both hands are in balance as in the overlapping grip, that is, with each **V** pointing to the center of the body.

Ten Finger Grip

In this grip, all ten fingers are in contact with the club. The hands should be placed as close as possible without crowding them. They should be in balance, with each V pointing to the center of the body.

It is preferable to call this grip the ten finger grip instead of the baseball grip because you hold a baseball bat at a right angle to the fingers and this cannot be when holding a golf club. Due to the angle at which the golf club is held when the clubhead is on the ground behind the ball, and the inclined plane on which it is swung, it must lay diagonally across the hands and fingers. If the club were held at a right angle to the fingers, it would be difficult and most uncomfortable to place the clubhead on the ground at the address position. The clubhead would have a tendency to approach the ball too high, resulting in topped shots.

When is the 10 Finger Grip Recommended?

Although my preferred grip is the overlapping grip, there are circumstances that make it more beneficial to the player to use the 10 finger grip.

Following are my reasons for using it:

1. Very young children—their hands are too little to use any other grip.

2. Adults with very short fingers.

3. Adults with very small hands.

4. Adults who have developed arthritis and using any other grip is rather painful.

As long as the hands are in balance as described, the 10 finger grip is a perfectly good way to hold the golf club.

Grip Pressure

Golfers are always much concerned with the amount of pressure they should use to hold the golf club and which fingers apply the greatest pressure. The same attitude should exist in taking the grip when using a golf club as when using a tennis racket, holding a pencil, or holding a ball you are going to throw. No one worries about which finger holds tighter or which fingers are responsible for doing one thing or another when holding any other tool. Why should we have this worry in golf? We should not have it, it is unnecessary.

All fingers should be used equally to get the best grip on a golf club. There should be a feel of oneness—*not two hands or ten fingers.* When the grip is first taken, the pressure used should be equal from the little finger of the high hand to the thumb and index finger of the low hand. This is static pressure—the club is at rest.

Once the club is swinging, the grip pressure moves up and down through the hands and fingers, based on the speed of the swing. The greater the speed, the greater the pressure in the high hand. Because this shift in pressure is inevitable and uncontrollable on the conscious level, it can never be exactly determined.

Should the grip pressure at the swing speed of 100 miles per hour be increased that 20% at the beginning of the swing, at the beginning of the forward swing, at the impact point? (Is this percentage correct? Should it be a different number? Who could ever tell?) Effort to determine such things keeps people from learning the game easily and quickly; it creates unnecessary complications that seriously affect your game.

Once the club is swinging, it creates a tremendous pull (centrifugal force), and it exerts the greatest pull on those fingers farthest from the clubhead, causing those fingers to grip tighter. The fingers farthest from the clubhead, of course, are the last three fingers of the high hand. For this change to take place, there must be motion and speed must be created. You cannot and must not attempt to make this pressure adjustment consciously, rather you must react naturally to the centrifugal force created by the speed of the swinging motion.

Practice Exercise

To better understand what all this means, take a club and hold it as though you were going to play a golf shot. Have someone pull the club while you are holding it and observe what happens to the pressure of your grip. It increases gradually in the last fingers of your high hand and decreases in the thumb and index finger of your low hand—the degree of change is directly proportional to the amount of pull. Now both of you stop pulling. Notice that as the degree of pull is less, the pressure in the last fingers of your high hand decreases until when the pull is zero, the pressure returns to what it was originally, before there was any pulling.

Notice that you did not try to determine consciously how you were going to change your grip pressure—*it just happened*.

Therefore, you will play better by maintaining an attitude of *constant* pressure in your grip. Many players have either experienced or witnessed a loosening of the pressure in the fingers of one or both hands as the club reaches the end of the backswing so that the palms become visible. This is lack of constant grip pressure. If this happens, you should not attempt to grip "harder" because even if you increase the grip pressure, if it does not remain constant, the hands can still open up.

Once the grip pressure has decreased at the end of the backswing, the player will regrip the club to prepare for the forward swing speed. This re-gripping twists the club, making it impossible to return the club to the proper square position at impact. Regripping the club at the beginning of the forward swing tends to cause a leverage action—casting—as the player attempts to swing the club forward.

Loosening the grip pressure at the end of the swing also occurs sometimes. The grip pressure at this point should be the same as it was at the beginning of the swing. There is no guarantee that this decrease in grip pressure will not happen earlier in the forward swing, and should it happen prior to ball contact, good shots will be very elusive.

The moral of this discussion is that your only concern in holding the golf club is to do just that: "hold it." Hold it with a constant attitude and allow the natural reactions to the swing to take place without interference on your part.

Another question often asked is: "How tightly should I hold the club?" There is no specific answer to this question. If I tell a group of players to hold the club lightly, *lightly* will not mean the same thing to all present. If I tell the same group to hold it firmly, *firmly* will not mean the same thing to all present. Both words are relative terms to each individual.

We can correlate how tightly to hold the golf club with holding other tools. For example, everyone has used a hammer at one time or another. No one has ever taken lessons in the use of one, and yet everyone does a rather good job hitting the nail, even though we may sometimes miss and hit our thumb. If you are trying to drive a small nail into a soft piece of wood, the hammer is held rather lightly *automatically*. However, if you are trying to drive a big nail into a very hard piece of wood, the power increase necessary to do this will make you hold the hammer much more firmly *automatically*. Your thoughts certainly are not on how much pressure is necessary or which fingers must hold more or less firmly.

You may say, well, a hammer is not a golf club, it cannot be handled the same way or its motion thought of in the same terms. It is true that they are different tools and are used for different purposes, but our attitude for making both motions should not differ. Prove it to yourself by trying to hit a nail worrying about holding the hammer tighter with the last three fingers of your hand and very lightly with the thumb and index finger. Be sure you get your other hand out of the way quickly.

So the pressure used should be directly proportional to the length of the club to be used and the speed with which it is going to be used. This varies with each individual. It further varies with the shots you wish to play. The grip of a delicate chip shot will automatically be much lighter than if a shot is going to be played out of heavy rough. *These adjustments are instinctive based on the job at hand.*

If your grip is lighter than it should be, it will be difficult for you to start the club swinging and will require a sudden tightening of your hands and fingers to make the club move. On the other hand, if your grip is tighter than necessary, it will create rigidity in your hands, wrists, forearms, arms, etc.. It will destroy clubhead feel, swing speed, and awareness, making it difficult to swing correctly. *Instinctively, players will determine what has to be done, and will determine their own pressure feel.*

The lie of the ball also affects the pressure needed to make the shot. A ball lying in heavy grass or buried in a bunker requires greater swing speed. Heavy grass tends to twist the clubhead as it approaches the ball, and in sand a buried ball requires more speed to get the sand iron deep enough to send the ball on its way. In both situations all players will hold the club more firmly.

These normal changes in grip pressure are the inevitable results of a player's preparation to execute the shot. *They are subconscious, and the instinctiveness with which they are made must be left instinctive.* Regardless of how players wish to consciously establish a particular grip pressure for what is being attempted, they will never be correct—their instinct is much wiser and accurate.

The human being is subject to many changes and moods. Everything we do is controlled and varied by them. Conscious control of the results of the changes and moods is most difficult. We are not always the same John Doe, sometimes we are happy, sometimes we are sad. Other times we are angry, other times we don't care. All of our activities are affected by these moods, and yet we cannot control the degree to which they affect us. Trying to do it consciously only makes it worse. We must accept that we are human beings and that human instincts are very effective.

Pressure and Feel

In order to swing properly, you must have clubhead feel. This means that you are aware of its mass, where it is, and how it is moving. To prove how hand and finger pressure can affect your clubhead feel, do this simple exercise.

Practice Exercise

Standing erect, hold a club directly in front of you so that the shaft is horizontal and the toe of the clubhead is pointing upward. Do this first with a very tight grip. You do not have much clubhead feel, do you? There seems to be no weight at the end of the shaft. Now lighten the grip and immediately the weight of the clubhead is very evident. In trying to swing an object (a golf club in this case), if you cannot feel it you cannot swing it because you are not aware of it.

How much you had to lighten the grip to become aware of the club-head weight only you could determine instinctively. No one can tell you.

Improving Your Grip

I certainly hope that all readers who have a defective grip will make the effort to improve it. Grip improvements should be made with small changes, a little at a time, so that the new feel will not be unacceptable to you.

Making small changes is very important because you can expect the following:

1. Your hands will feel somewhat different. Unfortunately, you will consider this difference uncomfortable.

2. Prior to the start of the swing, your hands will attempt to regrip the club the old way in search of the "comfortable feel."

3. If the defect in the grip is very severe, and the grip is changed 100%, the ball may at first react by going in the opposite direction. That is, if you have been slicing, you might now develop a hooking shot. If you were hooking you might now develop a slice. Changes of this magnitude can be very distressing.

4. The motion of the club (the swinging motion) will have an entirely different feel. This difference should not be interpreted as a "terrible feel," as so often happens. It is simply different, and must be considered in this light.

You should consider all of these points the price of change and improvement. Improving your grip takes great persistence. It is imperative that you accept every one of the above four points and work on the correction in spite of them but, remember, *gradually*.

If you attempt to change your grip to 100% perfect all at once, and it is a big change, all four points could be augmented to such a degree that you will say and even believe "I can't do it that way." Of course, no such statement is ever true, anything can be done if the person is willing, but your mental attitude will resist the change. The difference is too great to be acceptable.

Adopt a good attitude for making necessary changes. A proper mental attitude is essential in anything we do, if we expect to succeed, thus, if you are changing your grip, don't say the new one feels bad or uncomfortable or terrible. This creates a negative mental attitude. No one likes or will try to do something that feels bad or uncomfortable—it is human nature. If this is your attitude, you will never make the change. Change this to a positive mental attitude by saying "Oh, so that is the way it is supposed to feel, it feels different." Your chances for improvement will be much better.

When changing your grip, point 2 will be the most troublesome—re-gripping—you will do it without being aware of doing it, as subconsciously you look for the comfortable feel in the hands. Regripping cancels the attempt to make the change so you must keep yourself from doing it. This helps: Do not place the clubhead on the ground behind the ball during the address prior to starting the backswing.

Gripping the Club Visually

Once you have achieved the correct grip, it must stay in the same position forever, it must never be changed or allowed to change. Why would anyone change the grip if it is correct? Because we as human beings feel different from time to time and because of this difference, the grip may not always feel "comfortable." In search of "comfort," we change our hands in some way. Should this happen, it will have a most serious effect on the swinging motion and clubhead position.

An example of an instance when we adjust and change our hands in search of comfort is on a very hot and humid day. Our fingers may feel swollen or puffy, and when we place our hands on the club, they feel uncomfortable as though our fingers cannot fit in the usual space. We tend to make an attempt to fit our hands in such a way that the discomfort is diminished. This must be prevented at all costs. How can it be prevented?

It is very simple. When you are learning to place the hands on the club correctly, you should always take the grip while looking at your hands to see how you are placing them on the club. During this learning period, you should be developing a very clear picture of how your hands look to you when on the club correctly. Thus, if your hands on some days feel as though they want to go on differently, look at them while taking the grip. *Position the hands visually* and use that grip even though at that particular time it may feel uncomfortable. After playing a few shots, whether on the practice tee or the golf course, you will find that whatever discomfort seemed to be present will disappear *and you will not have changed your grip*.

If your grip changes, you are on your way to trouble even though you have not started to swing. Be very concerned and check your grip every time you hold your club. Look at your hands as you are placing them on the club. This does not mean once a week, or once a month, but constantly, every time you hold a golf club.

Your grip controls the position of the clubhead at all times. Exercise great care in learning or correcting your grip and exercise great care in keeping it right and always the same. It will pay you dividends.

Summary

1. Place your hands on the golf club in balance with relation to each other and to the target line, with each **V** pointing to the center of the body.

2. Grip with equal pressure in all fingers.

3. Maintain a constant pressure attitude throughout the golf swing.

4. Allow your instinct to determine your grip pressure.

5. If grip improvement changes are made, make them very gradually.

6. Place the hands on your club visually so they will always be the same.

Chapter 2

The Address Position

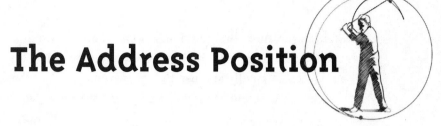

Once you have placed your hands on the club, you must approach the ball. The positioning of the club behind the ball followed by the positioning of the body square to the club face is called taking the stance or setting the address position. It is imperative that you feel perfectly comfortable and balanced after taking the stance. It is not necessary to go into contortions as is so commonly done just to simply place the clubface behind the golf ball and face it squarely. You must approach this positioning just the same as if someone was holding his hand out and you were asked to place the clubhead in his hand. You would not stiffen the arms or bend the knees or change the weight on the feet or any of the many other things that golfers tend to think about to do this simple thing.

The following steps are necessary to take the proper stance and address position:

1. Place the clubhead behind the golf ball so that:

   a. The clubhead not the ball is in the center between your feet (this is the same for all clubs and for all normal shots, ie, those that have normal height and are directed straight to the target).

   b. The end of the shaft (grip end) points to the center of the body. See Figure 10.

Definition of the Center: *The center between the feet is not determined by bisecting the distance between the toes. It is determined by the vertical line from the midpoint between the shoulders to the ground. Where that line touches the ground is the center between the feet and that is where the clubhead of all clubs should be placed. See Figures 9a and 9b.*

---

2. Position the body so that:

   a.   The shoulders, if they were level, would be parallel to the target line. Since the shoulders are not level, they should be on the same plane as the target line.

   b.   The shaft of the club bisects the **V** formed by the arms.

   c.   The body faces the clubface squarely.

   d.   The weight is equally divided between the feet.

   e.   The weight is evenly divided on each foot—it should not be on the heels. You should feel it on the balls of the feet.

Besides feeling comfortable and natural, you should have a good sense of balance. Balance is extremely important in any type of movement of an object and it is no less important in golf. Poor balance in your address position will give you a poor start.

Some individuals need a bit of help in finding good balance and the following exercise is most helpful.

Figure 9a　　　　　*Figure 9b*　　　　　*Figure 10*

Finding Good Balance

Practice Exercise

1. Take a stance you feel is in balance.

2. Close your eyes and do the rest of the exercise with your eyes closed.

3. Straighten your body so it is perfectly erect and have the club out in front of you with the shaft of the club in a horizontal position.

4. While in this erect position, move the club to the right or left.

5. Bring the club back to a horizontal level directly in front of you. Do not push the club away from you or try to keep it close to you. Be as natural as you can.

6. Now bend forward until the clubhead touches the ground.

Open your eyes and check to see where the clubhead is in relation to your feet. If it is in the center, and if the tip of the shaft points to the center of your body, you will be in perfect balance. See Figure 10.

If you find that this is not the case, repeat the exercise several times. If you continue to have difficulty in finding your balance, do the exercise in front of a mirror. Face it squarely, and when you complete step 5, open your eyes and check to see if the shaft of the club you are holding and its mirror image are in a straight line. If they are not, you are not in balance, so make the adjustment necessary to achieve the straight line and proceed with step 6.

I am certain that everyone knows that a person does not feel the same every day, does not do the same things exactly the same each time. Human beings are just not machines. In golf this also happens—there are small variations that are uncontrollable and normal. The width of the stance may vary somewhat from day to day. Because of this, placing the clubhead in the center of the stance becomes a very important factor. Regardless of how the width of the stance may change, if the clubhead is in the center of the stance, the changes in width will not affect the swing at all.

Here is a summary of what can happen when the position of the club-head is shifted to the right or left of center.

1. **Clubhead placed to the left of center** (right-handed players).

   a. Club will be swung back to the outside of the target line.

   b. Shoulder line points to the left (crossing the target line).

   c. The direction of the forward swing will be across the target line to the left.

   d. The ball will have a tendency to start toward the left with or without a slicing spin.

The degree of severity of each of the above depends on how much the clubhead is moved to the left. The farther from center, the greater the reaction.

2. **Clubhead moved to the right of center** (right-handed players).

   a. Club will be swung back too far inside.

   b. Shoulder line points to the right.

   c. The direction of the forward swing will be across the target line to the right.

   d. The ball will have a tendency to start to the right with or without a hooking spin.

Again, the degree of severity depends upon how much the clubhead has been moved from the center toward the right.

If you change the clubhead location toward the left of center at address but keep the position of your body as though the clubhead were in the center, the shaft of the club will be pointing toward your right side while the clubhead points to the left. From this position, the movement of your body and the swinging motion of the club will be at odds with each other in relation to the direction in which the ball is to be propelled. The body is set to move toward the target, but the club is set to move to the left.

If you do the opposite—place the clubhead to the right of center but hold your body position as though the clubhead were centered, the shaft of the club will be pointing to your left side. Again, the movements of the body and club will not be compatible. The body is set to move toward the target and the club is set to swing to the right.

Four very detrimental arm and hand positions are practiced by a large number of golfers:

1. Club as an extension of the left arm.

2. Hands ahead of the clubhead and ball.

3. Left arm is straight while the right arm and elbow are bent and below the left arm.

4. Elbows are turned so that they are pointed downward and are close to each other.

It is difficult to imagine anything that will make a player more uncomfortable and unnatural than those four ideas. Why should it be necessary to be so contorted just to place the head of a golf club next to the golf ball? The next time you are with a friend, have that person hold a golf club and ask that the clubhead be placed in your hand, which you extend toward that person. What do you notice? The opposite of those four ideas above:

1. The person's left arm and golf club are *not* an extension of each other. The shaft bisects the **V** formed by the arms.

2. The person's hands are *not* ahead of the clubhead, they are even with it.

3. The person's right arm and elbow are *not* below the straight left arm because both arms are bent and about even with each other.

4. The person's elbows are not pointed straight down and they are not particularly close to each other.

If this simple and natural attitude is good enough to put the clubhead in someone's hand, it should be good enough to place it at the ball. If the hand were on the ground behind the golf ball, would we now act differently if we placed the clubhead on it? Certainly not.

Remember that anything you do that is not natural will bring difficulty to your attempt to make a good dependable and repetitive golf swing.

Width of Stance

How wide should your stance be? This varies with each individual, and the circumstances surrounding the execution of a particular shot also make variations in width necessary. The width should be such that you feel that whatever has to be done can be done without strain, remaining in good balance throughout the swing as well as at the end of the swing.

A player who has long legs and a short trunk will and should take a wider stance than a player who has a long trunk and short legs. A player who is rather stout will find it easier to make a good swing with a narrower stance, while a slender player will be the opposite.

A player attempting to swing the club with very high acceleration will widen his or her stance, and one attempting a short delicate shot will narrow the stance. Therefore, using the driver will automatically make the player use a fairly wide stance, thus creating a greater base to handle the tremendous force created by swinging that club pretty close to the maximum potential.

The mental awareness of what you are going to do will instinctively set your base.

It is not necessary to place a minimum limit (narrowness) of the stance because the player's feel will control this adequately, but there is a need to place a maximum limit (width). Assuming the swing is correct, the limitation is: If you find it difficult to have your body respond in the backswing or to have your weight transfer to your front foot after impact, your stance is too wide. This weight transfer should occur naturally and without strain.

As you see, it is difficult to set a fast rule, but there has to be a starting point, and a general rule is to start with a stance about the width of your shoulders.

Types of Stances

There are three types of stances.

1. Square: The line from toe to toe is parallel to the target line.

2. Open: There are two types.

   a. If you want to strike the ball squarely (with no spin) but feel more comfortable with an open stance, retract your front foot from the target line so that the line from toe to toe points to the left. The front foot, however, will be at the same angle to the target line as the back foot.

   This type of open stance maintains the shoulders on the same plane as the target line—they will not be pointing to the left.

   b. If you want to strike the ball with a slicing tendency, retract your front foot from the target line so that the line from toe to toe points to the left of the target line. The front foot in this stance will be at a greater angle to the target line, turned out toward the target. This makes the shoulder line point to the left—the shoulders will be open. This type of open stance restricts the backswing and also forces the club to be swung in a more upright plane in the backswing and to the left across the line on the forward swing.

3. Closed: There are two types.

   a. If you want to strike the ball squarely (with no spin) but feel more comfortable with a closed stance, retract your back foot from the target line so that the line from toe to toe points to the right. The back foot, however, should be at the same angle to the target line as the front foot.

   This type of closed stance will maintain the shoulders on the same plane as the target line.

   b. If you want to strike the ball with a hooking tendency, retract your back foot from the target line so that the line from toe to toe points to the right of the target line. The back foot in this stance will be at a greater angle to the target line, turned away from the target and the shoulder line will point to the right.

Note: *In Chapter 10, Unusual Shots, hooking and slicing are discussed. A different method, not requiring a change in stance to accomplish different ball flight patterns will be demonstrated.*

Weight Distribution and Posture

A good sense of balance requires equal distribution of weight on your feet, that is, 50% of your total weight on each foot. This weight must also be equally distributed on the feet front to back. Remember that we are discussing requirements for normal straight shots, from level lies. Other situations and requirements for special situations will be discussed in Chapter 10 on Unusual Shots.

Greater amount of weight on the front foot will make you pick up the club too vertically and make it difficult to swing the club backward and forward. The resulting shots will be very low shots with a tendency to make the ball slice and the divots will be rather deep.

If there is too much weight on the back foot, it will be more difficult to transfer your weight to the front foot in the forward swing. This can cause the club to be swung upward resulting in topped shots and can also cause you to hit the ground behind the ball.

In both cases, having more weight on one foot than the other causes inconsistent results.

Posture is a very individual thing. No matter how hard we try, we cannot look like someone else while performing like tasks. No two people look the same when they are walking, running, or doing anything else you can think of. So why, in golf should there be such an effort to look like someone else? Most of the things people do from the standpoint of posture are imitations of personal and individual characteristics.

When you place the clubhead behind the golf ball, be yourself and look like yourself. This means be natural. Don't stick any part of your body out in any direction if it doesn't usually stick out. All you will

33

accomplish is to look odd, and this look will be passed on to your swing—it will look odd and be most inefficient.

Your knees should have normal flex. Anytime you flex your knees beyond what is normal for you, the body turn necessary to remain synchronized with the club in the backswing is decreased, especially if your knees stay in that exaggerated flexed position.

If we are playing tennis, baseball, or running, the exaggerated flexed position is necessary because we are going to spring forward or sideways and run. But where are we going when we swing a golf club? Nowhere. Golf is a rotational sport and as we swing the golf club, we turn around a center line, so we must act in a way that allows us to do this.

I ask all of my students who have an exaggerated knee flex why they do it, and they invariably say, "I am trying to feel relaxed." Being relaxed means that there is no muscular tension, so to test how relaxed you are, feel your thigh muscles when you bend your knees to excess. Those muscles are hard and contracted. If they were not, you would fall down. Bending the knees beyond your normal does not produce a relaxed condition.

When the hips turn in the backswing, they will tend to straighten the backswing side leg—it will not lock back but it will have a tendency to straighten. This is the normal way the body responds to the type of turning motion produced in the backswing and allows the player to make a very full turn.

An athletic position at address is that which allows your body to move with great ease throughout the golf swing, not just in the backswing. The exaggerated knee bend is certainly not the way to achieve this naturalness and ease.

Chapter 3

Alignment

To propel the golf ball to the target, the player must align the clubface and the body in such a way as to enable the swinging motion to be produced in the direction of that target with ease.

Alignment is a rather simple procedure and it starts with placing the clubhead behind the ball so that the face is at a right angle to the target line.

Once you feel certain that the clubface is aimed properly but before you move to take your stance, focus on the clubface so that when you start to move to take your stance, the clubface remains motionless. Do not raise the clubhead off the ground while moving to take the stance—your clubface alignment will change. If you notice that the clubface has moved, the entire procedure should be repeated.

Once you have done this, take your stance by facing the clubface squarely. This places your shoulders on the same plane as the target line; if they were level they would be parallel to it.

Many times a player will take an incorrect alignment to make allowances for undesirable ball flights.

- If there is a tendency for the player to slice, the alignment will be set to the left.

- If there is a tendency for the player to hook, the alignment will be set to the right.

These allowances are very disturbing to the swing because the player must then produce a slice or hook in order to send the ball down the fairway, intensifying his or her difficulty in sending the ball straight to the target. If the player does make a good swing and send the ball straight, it will be well off the target.

Checking Alignment

Be as careful in your alignment procedure as you are in holding the club properly. Check it often, as improper alignment will alter your swing and the position of the clubhead at impact. To check your alignment, you need someone to help you. Follow this procedure:

Practice Exercise

1. Take your normal stance with a target in mind.

2. Have someone take your place and hold the grip end of the club, simply having it rest on that person's open hand.

3. Move to a point directly behind the clubhead and check to see where the clubface is aimed.

4. Change the clubface alignment if incorrect.

5. Retake your stance with the correct alignment, being very careful not to change the new alignment when taking your grip. Keep your eye on the club face.

6. Observe the difference.

> **Warning:** *When changing the alignment of the clubface do not just rotate the clubhead because this will open or close the face. The entire club must be moved when realigning the clubface.*

Repeat the above procedure several times because if the alignment has been incorrect for a while, it will feel different when corrected.

Sometimes our alignment changes because our eyes for some reason fail to see the right angle between the target line and face of the club. The reason for this is difficult to explain, but it does happen. Thus we need to continually check our alignment to lessen the chance of damaging the swing through improper alignment.

All golfers have at one time or another experienced doubt as to whether or not they are lined up correctly. Many times there is no problem, but it just does not feel correct. Checking your alignment as previously suggested should satisfy you. What happens when the alignment is correct but the player doubts it, because of a change in the feel? During the execution of the swing, the player makes definite manipulations in order to correct something that is not there. Results will not be good. The worse part of this doubt is the confusion it creates in the player's mind, and it is not easy to do something well when there is mental confusion.

Never take your alignment for granted—it is sensitive to the way we feel and the way we observe.

Methods for Taking Alignment

A method used by some players is to set up the toe line in line with the target. Other players like to set up so that if the shoulders were level, the shoulder line would point to the target. Both of these methods produce an alignment that will be way to the right of their target.

Practice Exercise

To prove this to your satisfaction, place a tee in the ground and use it as your target. Place a golf ball about 3 feet away from the tee and take your address position lining up your toe line to the tee, place a club on the ground touching your toes and pointing to the tee. Now check to see where the clubface of the club with which you are addressing the ball is aiming. It is not at the tee is it? It is way to the right.

A second method is to use an intermediate target and line up the clubface to it, hoping that because the intermediate target is much closer than the actual target, it will be easier to line up the clubface properly. This method is perfectly fine if the intermediate target is really on the target line.

An intermediate target is one on the ground about 2 or 3 feet from the location of the golf ball. If this target is selected properly, it must be on the actual target line. To check if you have done this correctly, place a tee in the spot where you have chosen to place your intermediate target. Then place a club over the tee and the other end of the club resting on the ball. Get behind the club and check to see if it is in line with your target. I find that when I make this check practically everyone is off to some degree, so it is not an infallible method. If upon checking your intermediate target in this manner, it is on the target line, then it may be of some help.

This third method is the recommended method—it is the most effective and consistent:

Stand behind the golf ball so that your eyes (actually it will be your master eye), the golf ball, and the target are on a straight line. Then do the following.

1. Look at your hands and grip the club properly.

2. With the club already held, walk at approximately 45 degrees to your left until you find yourself even with the golf ball.

3. **Do not take your eye off your target while walking to the ball.**

4. When reaching the ball you should be facing the target, *not the ball.*

5. Take a step with your right foot and have it point toward the ball.

6. Place the clubface behind the ball keeping your eye on the target until the last possible moment.

7. Check to see that the clubface is aiming where you want to go, if not, reset the clubface.

8. Up to this point you have not taken a stance.

9. When you feel sure of your alignment, look at your clubface and check to see that when you move your feet to take your stance, *you do not allow your clubface to move or you will change your aim.*

10. Take your stance and place your body in general square to the club-face. Do not focus on your feet or your shoulders or your hips. Act as though you were trying to face a person squarely.

When you first start to use this method, it may seem somewhat tedious and lengthy, but as you get used to it, you will do it all with one purpose and within your rhythm. It will become very natural.

The secret in this method is keeping your eye on the target as long as possible. If you get behind the ball to get your line and then look at the ball as you start to walk toward the ball, you will lose your line.

When checking the setup in the third method you will find that when the clubface is aimed at the target, the shoulder line will be on the same plane as the target line. Or, if the shoulders were level, the shoulder line would be parallel to the target line. The toe line, if you have a square stance, will also be parallel to the target line, but left of the target (or to the right for left-handed players).

The setup to attain proper stance and alignment is extremely important because a very small change in the alignment of the clubface produces great distortion in the direction of the shot when this change is projected forward. Only 2 degrees variation in the clubface position translates into approximately 40 feet at 200 yards.

Practice Exercise

Form a **V** with the index finger and the middle finger of your hand, spread them as far as you can. Now aim your index finger at an object and notice where the middle finger is pointing. The farther away your target is, the farther away from it the middle finger points.

If you are the type of player who places the clubface behind the ball with the feet together, you must remember to spread your feet by moving your right foot first. If the left foot is moved first the clubface aim will be changed and it will be aiming to the right. Left-handed players who have their feet together when placing the clubface behind the ball must move their left foot first when taking their stance. Moving the right foot first changes the clubface aim to the left.

Once you have aligned yourself and taken your stance, if you have the slightest doubt in your mind as to whether you are right or wrong, do not adjust. Go through the entire procedure all over again. When adjusting, it is very easy to overdo it, so things may get worse instead of better. Regardless of your feel for your line, even if lined up correctly, any doubt that may exist in your mind about it will affect your ability to perform your swing correctly.

Part II

Visualizing the Swing

Chapter 4

Analyzing the Swing

In this chapter we discuss the development of a true swinging motion of the club. Recall also that our concept maintains that if you produce a true swinging motion with the golf club, body positions so often described and emphasized will happen naturally. If the body is allowed to be responsive, the movement of the body will be compatible and correct.

Responsiveness of the Body to the Swing

For this section you may also refer back to page 7, **The Swing—The Most Important Concept**. Let's analyze the points presented there in more detail.

1. *Left Arm Straight.* What does keeping the left arm (right arm for left-handed players) straight mean? Is it the same for everyone? Will everyone interpret those words to mean the same thing?

   When a player attempts to keep the left or right arm straight, it is kept straight through rigidity. Once this rigidity exists, it has to be released on the forward swing. But where should it be released? No one can say where. Usually, that rigidity is maintained much too long, causing the clubhead to be open at impact and slicing is the result. The backswing also tends to get shorter, so distance is further decreased.

   The left arm extends in the backswing and the right arm bends, the right arm extends in the forward swing and the left arm bends (reverse for left-handed players). Both of these facts are reactions to the swing. The player should make no effort to bend the arms or keep them straight.

   If a right-handed player would swing as a left-handed player swings, it would be easy to see how the left arm bends in the backswing of a left-handed player, which is the forward swing of a right-handed player.

If a player collapses the left arm (right arm for a left-handed player) at the end of the backswing, thereby breaking the swing radius, it could create some difficulties. To correct it, the player should sense that the hands remain as far as possible from him at the end of the backswing. As the club reaches the end of the backswing, the hands should not move toward the player's head. This will maintain the arm extension, but since the attention is not on the arm, no rigidity will be created.

2. *Looking Up.* Looking up or "peeking" is such a wonderful excuse for a missed shot. How acceptable it is for everyone Players who feel that this is the reason they miss shots, make such an effort to keep the head down but continue to miss the shots anyway.

Keeping the head down consciously destroys the freedom of the shoulder and general body response in the forward swing. The shoulders go into a tilting attitude and the body bends excessively backward which can and does cause severe back problems. Clubwise, the clubhead will tend to be open, thus, slicing comes into the picture again.

The player should keep his or her eyes on the ball and follow it in the same natural way it is done in baseball, tennis, or ping pong. Why should it be any different in golf? It should not.

When the eyes are fixed on an object, it is impossible for them to change that fixed vision suddenly when something moving at a high rate of speed goes by and crosses that fixed vision line. By the time the eyes move to search for the moving object, it will be well past them. Thus, *it is impossible to look up.* If a shot is missed, the player did something to the swing and that is what has to be corrected. Keeping the head down could make things worse instead of better—it will not fix the problem.

3. *Weight Transfer.* Does weight transfer happen in everyone's swing to the same degree and in the same way? Is the weight distribution at impact time the same for all players? What about the differences in width of stance? What about a person who is very slender compared with one who is not?

The transfer of weight cannot be described in a step by step manner. Does any player know the rate at which his weight must transfer in order to match his club speed? No one knows this so a player who consciously tries to transfer his weight will most likely transfer it too fast, too slowly, prematurely, or too late, resulting in the ball tending to slice.

Practice Exercise

Stand as if you were addressing a golf ball, then take a ball and throw it underhand as far as you can down the fairway and hold your finish. Observe where your weight is. Did you make any effort to transfer your weight? It has transferred naturally to the front foot without any help from you. This is the way the weight should transfer in your golf swing.

4. *Right Elbow Close to the Body.* When a player makes it a point to get the right elbow close to the body as the club is swung forward from the beginning of the forward swing, the club will be forced into a very flat plane. It cannot remain in the plane on which that player should be swinging and which was set at the address position.

5. *Pulling the Club.* A pulling action doesn't work. The golf swing is a circular motion. However. the force used to pull or push any object can only be applied in a straight line. So when a player attempts to use a pulling action, a straight line component is introduced into a motion that is circular. *It will not work because it destroys the swing.*

6. *Wrist Action.* When a good player or one who obtains great distance is observed, the comment is often made: "Look at his wrist action." The observation is correct, but when the observer goes to the practice tee to work on that wrist action, what he or she produces is hand action, not wrist action.

When the hands become active as the clubhead approaches the ball, it is impossible, except by chance, to have the clubhead at a right angle to the target line at impact. The player will develop a tremendous variety of bad shots. *Wrist action is developed through arm speed and flexibility,* not hand action.

From this analysis, the reader should clearly see that being concerned with so many details would make success an impossible task. Bear in mind that these six points are just a few samples of what goes on in a player's mind. The truth is that the details that concern the players are so numerous that it would be impossible to list and discuss them without writing an enormous book.

Golf is a wonderful game and it should be enjoyed more than it is. It is not difficult to swing the golf club and have it strike the golf ball in a manner that is satisfying. Six-year-old children have little trouble and their minds are not full of all kinds of strange ideas. How can a child develop so quickly using imitation and very simple language? Why should adults become so complicated and analytical of every inch of the swing and have such difficulties with it?

A child does not care why things happen or do not happen. If they miss a shot they simply try again. An adult misses a shot and has to know the reason for the miss, immediately creating a need to change something.

This experimentation with change will not produce repetitive sound swings.

I want you to understand the golf swing, but in the end you will see that the golf swing can be approached by adults with that childlike simplicity.

A golf club can be moved by using two different types of motions:

- Swinging motion

- Leverage action

Why is the motion used in golf always referred to as a swing? What is the difference between a leverage action and a swinging motion? Which should be used in golf and why?

The Character of a True Swinging Motion

1. Within a given arc, a swinging motion produces the greatest amount of speed possible.

2. In a swinging motion, everything in motion moves in the same direction at the same time and at the same rate.

3. The forces used to produce a swinging motion have only one direction, and because of this, great speeds can be generated.

4. A true swinging motion creates centrifugal force. The greater the speed of the swing the greater the centrifugal force.

Leverage Action

In a leverage action, two forces exist, but they have opposite directions. This type of action is very powerful to move heavy objects, but it cannot generate velocity.

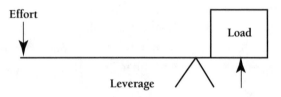

Forces working in opposite directions do not generate optimal speed.

Let's look at an example of forces working in opposite directions:

Suppose we have two horses of equal power and a cart to which they can be attached. If we attach one horse to one side of the cart and the other one to the opposite side, and then we make both go as fast as they can, how fast will the cart be going? It would be standing absolutely still. The power of one horse cancels the power of the other one. Now if we attach both horses to the same side of the cart, the cart can really go, because both horses are moving in the same direction.

In golf, we have to generate velocity, so everything involved has to move in the same direction at the same time and at the same rate. When the hands are used to hit the ball, opposite forces are generated with a great loss of speed. With the hands used to produce the "hit," the clubhead moves forward but the butt end of the club shaft moves backward, slows down , or stays still. See Figure 22a, p. 129. This results in leverage action.

Identifying the Swinging Motion

The word swing has been part of the golf terminology ever since the game has been played, but, unfortunately, golfers do not know how to identify it. Before it can be identified, it has to be felt, it has to be sensed.

Practice Exercise

If we attach a weight to a piece of string and move the string back and forth, a swinging motion is the result. To transfer this movement to the golf swing, when gripping the golf club, the string can be placed within the grip so that the string and the golf club are held at the same time. Now move the club back and forth and keep the weight at the end of the string and the club moving together. This is a swinging motion. This is the sensation a player should have when swinging a golf club. When doing this exercise, only a 180 degree arc should be used so that the club only reaches a horizontal position half way in the backswing and half way to the end of the swing after impact. Once this swinging motion is felt and recognized, it can be imparted to the golf club through the entire golf swing. See Figures 11, 12, 13, and 14.

When doing this exercise, your mind was on only one thing. Keeping the club and the weight on the string moving in unison. It was not on your head, hips, knees, or feet.

Hold the club now without the string and make the same swinging motion you made with the club and the string. Once the club is swung away from the ball, the club must remain swinging backward and forward regardless of the size of the swing.

What would using leverage have done to this exercise? Had leverage been applied to start the club moving, the clubhead would have moved, but the weight on the string would have remained motionless hanging vertically.

Visualizing the Golf Club In Motion

In order to swing the club effectively, we must know how the clubhead and the shaft should look while in motion, thus developing a mental picture of the correct movement. Being able to "see" the following images will develop that mental picture.

Figure 11

Figure 12

Figure 13

Figure 14

1. A swinging motion is a circular motion. It contains no straight lines, so no effort should be made to swing the club straight back or straight forward.

2. When the club reaches a horizontal position halfway in the backswing, the shaft of the club should be parallel to the target line and the toe of the clubhead should be pointing to the sky.

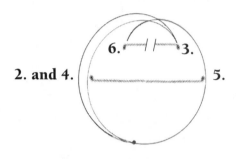

3. If, and when, the club reaches the horizontal position at the end of the backswing, the shaft of the club should be parallel to the target line and the toe of the clubhead should be pointing downward. It will not be vertical to the ground because of the inclined plane on which the golf club is being swung.

4. When the club reaches the horizontal position in the forward swing, halfway between the end of the backswing and the golf ball, the shaft of the club should be parallel to the target line and the toe of the clubhead should be pointing to the sky.

5. When the club reaches a horizontal position as it points forward after contacting the golf ball, the shaft of the club should be parallel to the target line and the toe of the clubhead should be pointing to the sky.

6. Finally, when the club reaches the horizontal position toward the end of the swing, the shaft of the club should be parallel to the target line and the toe of the clubhead should be pointing downward.

These "freeze-frame" positions are a matter of geometry. Anytime there is a circle, it is on a plane. All the horizontal chords of that circle are parallel to each other and to the tangent on that plane that represents the target line. In a golf swing, any time the golf club reaches a horizontal level, it becomes a partial chord of the circle described by the golf club.

Between the club's horizontal positions halfway in the backswing and halfway in the forward swing, the clubhead must be returned to the ball square to the target line.

By now, a very clear picture, a mental image, of a golf club in its swinging motion should be developing. As you produce this swinging motion, it will become very apparent that everything mentioned will happen naturally and properly if two conditions are met:

First, if the player swinging the club does not interfere in any way with the swinging motion,

Second, if the grip on the club is a balanced grip (see Chapter 1, on The Grip.)

What To Do To Produce the Swing

It is unfortunate that the golf swing is thought of as such a complicated and unnatural movement. The golf swing is such a simple movement and we humans complicate it to such an extent that it does not work. Our movement in the golf swing is essentially the same as many other everyday motions—the only difference is that in golf we do it with an implement called a golf club.

Backswing

To produce the backswing, the player must swing the clubhead back with the hands (both hands) toward the right shoulder so that when the backswing is completed, the club is over the shoulder. The hands must be used because a coil has to be created in order to be able to generate the desired speed. The hands must be used exclusively to swing the clubhead from the ball to the end of the backswing, where the arms take over and swing the entire club to the end of the swing.

When your hands swing the clubhead in the backswing, be sure that as soon as the clubhead starts to move, everything moves with it. Clubhead and shoulders start together, stay together, and reach the end of the backswing together. The rest of the body will respond automatically if it is relaxed.

Notice that when referring to hands and arms, the plural is used. Both hands are used in the backswing and both arms are used in the forward swing.

If a player would take the address position and lift the club vertically to place it on the shoulder, the hands would be used to make this movement. No other part of the body would be considered.

You should make no effort to cock your wrists in the backswing. When a player attempts to cock the wrists, they must be cocked in the plane that corresponds to the club being swung. This would be just another "moving part" making the golf swing difficult to produce.

The wrists are cocked by the club being swung over the shoulder. It is a natural reaction to that motion. It just happens.

Many players eliminate the use of the low hand in the backswing thereby making the high hand responsible for the backswing. This results in a high hand dominant backswing, causing the club to be laid off with the shaft pointing way to the right of the target and the clubhead facing the sky. See Figure 15.

Use both hands in order to make a good backswing.

The body or the arms could never swing the club so it would end up over the shoulder. Extra motions would have to be injected into the backswing in order to get the club to be over the shoulder. Extra motions complicate what is really a simple movement and make it difficult to perform.

Figure 15

Forward Swing

First a definition: The *arm* is that portion of the extremity from the shoulder to the elbow, the rest of it to the wrist is the *forearm*. Once the player reaches the end of the backswing, the responsibility for the rest of the motion (the forward swing) belongs to the arms. The arms then swing the entire club to the end of the swing in one uninterrupted motion. The arms through their speed are responsible for maintaining the coil produced by the hands in the backswing. This coil should be maintained as long as possible without creating any tension. The coil enables the golfer to generate maximum speed. The greater the arm speed, the longer the coil will be retained. When the arm speed cannot be increased, golfers have reached the limit of their distance. When the hands are used in the forward swing, the coil is *destroyed*, and the arms will slow down thereby decreasing the swing speed as well.

The clubhead is the leader of the backswing but in the forward swing it becomes the follower. It follows the arms as the club is returned to its starting position. The club, not just the clubhead, must be returned to its position at address. Unless this is accomplished, it is impossible to propel the golf ball in a straight line to the target and *only the arms can do this*.

The hands can produce a great number of different motions with the golf club, however, the arms, once they start the forward swing can only produce one—a consistent, effective, and satisfying swing. Casting is the result of using the hands or forearms at any point in the forward swing prior to contact, not just at the beginning of the forward swing.

Hands and Hand Action

Using the hands in the forward swing is the most common and the most detrimental type of motion used by golfers. Why is it so common? The answer is simple. Everyone is trying to generate clubhead speed in order to "hit" the golf ball. In order to increase distance, the golfer should try to increase the arm speed. If the speed is in the arms, it will automatically be present in the entire club, including the clubhead.

Hand action in the forward swing is the cause of more than 90% of all missed shots. When hand action is used in the forward swing, a leveraging type of motion is injected into the forward swing, destroying the swing.

If the hands are so detrimental to the swing, what then is the function of the hands in the forward swing?

1. They are used to hold the club.

2. They are used to control the club.

3. They passively transmit to the club the motion the arms are producing.

Using the hands at the beginning of the forward swing represents an effort from the player to get the clubhead back to the ball (this is a casting action) instead of returning the entire club.

Using the hands as the clubhead approaches the ball represents a desire by the player to control ball flight and/or apply power at that point to get more distance. Everyone has a tendency to try to help the club as it reaches the golf ball—*The swing will never accept this help.*

These efforts to use the hands in the forward swing interfere with the arms carrying out their responsibility. Once the forward swing has been initiated, it must be left alone to do the work it is supposed to accomplish.

In order to acquire the hand passiveness required for a good swing, there has to be *trust* in what the player has decided to do, and it must not be changed on the way to the end of the swing. Otherwise there will be a change in purpose. An excellent way to enhance this passiveness is to not allow the pressure in the grip to increase anywhere in the forward swing.

What does changing the purpose mean? It means to do something different while the swing is in progress from what the player had in mind prior to starting the swing.

At this point, let us make a comparison between hand action and wrist action.

Wrists and Hands

Practice Exercise

Extend your arm comfortably in front of you. Move your hand from right to left—this is *hand action,* just what the words imply. You are moving your hand but notice that your arm did not move. Your wrist acted merely as a hinge to *permit* you to move your hand.

Now, with the arm in the same position, permit your hand to dangle completely relaxed. Move your arm from left to right rapidly while your hand remains in that relaxed state. This produces *wrist action*—you are not doing anything with your hand.

We see this wrist action when we watch the good players, but we interpret it as *hand action*. When trying to duplicate what we observe—we go to the practice tee to work at it, but what we produce is hand action not wrist action.

Warning: When a player is told that the problem is hand interference in the forward swing, the first thing that player does is to stiffen the wrists to avoid the hand action. This is not the correct interpretation of the solution to the problem. The wrists must be kept free to hinge and unhinge when the motion of the club demands it.

Wrist action is an automatic and involuntary reaction of the hinge called wrist to the uncoiling action of the club in the forward swing, as a response to the centrifugal force developed through the swinging motion.

Arm Use In Other Activities

If we play tennis, the racquet is moved with the arm. If the power of the forehand is to be increased, the arm is moved faster. The hand is not used.

If you are dining and having a steak, and you use a knife to cut the steak, you will use the arm to move the knife. The hand is not used.

If you are driving an automobile and have to turn the steering wheel, you turn it with your arms. The hands are not used.

If you are cutting down a tree with an axe, you apply power with your arms. The hands are not used.

If you are trying to drive a post into the ground, you apply power with your arms. The hands are not used.

I could go on and on citing examples of arm use in our daily life when power and speed are necessary. Let us not change the normal because we are using a golf club.

In all these examples, the hands are used to hold on to the implement we are trying to use, and to keep it under control. They pass on to the implement used whatever motion the arms are producing. The same principle applies to the use of the golf club on the forward swing.

Wrists and hands are not synonymous words. The wrists are hinges that permit the individual to move his or her hands. When golfers are told they are using their hands, they have a great tendency to freeze the wrists to eliminate the hand use. The fact that the arms should be used in the forward swing instead of the hands does not imply that the wrist action, which must be present in the golf swing, has to be eliminated. Although the hands are not used, the wrists must remain free to permit the golf club to work properly in the forward swing.

To conclude:

Swing the clubhead back with the hands and swing the entire golf club forward with the arms from the beginning of the forward swing to the finish of the swing in one uninterrupted motion in the direction of your target.
If an increase in distance is desired, increase your arm speed not your clubhead speed. If your arms have it, your clubhead will have it automatically.

A Pause at the End of the Backswing?

When the club changes direction at the end of the backswing, it stops momentarily to make this change. Any object swinging back and forth on the same plane will do this. If I ask a person to walk away from me and return to me walking over the same footprints, that person would have to stop to change direction.

The player should make no effort to stop or pause at the end of the backswing. It just happens.

Players who do not use the same plane for both the backswing and the forward swing do not have this pause because it is not needed.

If a player attempts to consciously pause at the end of the backswing, the mental and physical purposes will be lost, thereby destroying the continuity between the backward and forward parts of the swing. The swing must never be split at any point either physically or mentally.

If a pause is deliberately developed by the player at the end of the backswing, there will be a tendency to slice the shot because the forward motion will be started with the shoulders. The ball will start to the left of the intended target and spin to the right (reversed for left-handed players).

When we throw a ball, do we make an effort to pause before the arm starts the forward motion? Would there be a conscious pause when playing tennis before moving the racquet forward? Would this be a consideration when hitting a baseball?

The answer is no. The change in direction may produce a momentary pause automatically—it is not produced intentionally.

In order to swing the golf club efficiently:

The mental and physical purpose or intent must be kept constant from the beginning of the swing to the end of the swing.

Important: *Swinging the clubhead with the hands in the backswing or swinging the entire club with the arms in the forward swing should not be interpreted as swinging the hands or swinging the arms. This interpretation will not produce a swinging motion with the club, which is what we are trying to accomplish. The hands and the arms are simply the vehicles used to produce the swinging motion of the club.*

What Should Move First?

In a golf swing nothing moves first. Everything moves at the same time (together) in the same direction and at the same rate. Just because the hands swing the clubhead back from the address position making the clubhead the leader, the clubhead does not and should not move first.

Just because the arms initiate and produce the forward swing making the clubhead the follower, the clubhead does not move last nor do the arms move first.

Once the hands or the arms initiate their respective movements, the body, if permitted, will respond to those movements the moment they are initiated.

If this response is not there, the hands and the arms will not be able to fulfill their responsibilities.

When we observe a good golfer, we always see a very striking unity between all parts of the body and club's motion. We see a whole, not parts—truly a fluid and effortless movement. This is the way you should visualize your own movement.

To Lead Does Not Mean To Move First

If we were watching a platoon of men marching, the men in the front row are the leaders, but when the marching command is given, they do not move first. Every man in the platoon moves at the same time.

Responsiveness

If a boy and girl are dancing (the type of dancing where the boy holds the girl), the boy is the leader, he initiates, he triggers the movement. The girl responds immediately as she senses the boy's leadership. If the boy moved first, meaning that the girl would move later, they certainly would have a difficult time. The boy and girl move simultaneously and those who are watching cannot really tell who is the leader, however, it would be easy to tell if one of them moved first.

The golf club is what is used to propel the golf ball, so everything that happens in the golf swing must be responsive to the club's motion. It is all one.

What About Body Motion?

The body moves a great deal in a golf swing, but it must be in direct response to the movement of the club. The body (shoulders, hips, knees, feet, etc.) should not be "used" to produce the swing but must move along with it.

No one can teach a person to respond, especially through body controlled movements, because the response to a stimulus is different in every human being. If a person makes a body motion consciously, then it is not really a response. The responsiveness of the body must be one that fits the individual concerned. Just because a favorite professional golfer makes a certain movement with his body, it does not mean that every golfer can or should make the same movement.

Even when walking, running or writing, each person does it differently, fitting the individuality and personality of that person. And an individual's own writing is not always the same—the same words written several times at the same sitting do not even look exactly the same.

Each person looks different and acts differently while doing the same things.

When it comes to golf, everyone wants to produce predetermined stereotyped body movements so that their movements can look like those of their idols. Professional golfers and golf instructors as well are guilty of this attitude. But this will never work. Watch the professionals in a golf tournament. No two players have the same swing responses body-wise, even though their clubs may be doing the same thing. If the professional players are this different, why should any player try to look exactly like them?

In looking at professionals, most observers will look at the body movements and not what the player does with the club being used.

Yet, the greatest and most helpful thing any golfer in any category should do when observing a good player is to study not what that player does with his or her body, but what that player does with the golf club, and the latter is what the observer should attempt to duplicate.

Do what the good players do with their golf club, but look like yourself while doing it.

What does a golf swing look like?

The golf swing is a composite of two circular motions that come very close to being perfect circles. The circle that corresponds to the forward swing is forward of the circle that corresponds to the backswing. See Figures 15a and 15c.

When the club is swung back from the ball and then returns to the ball, the paths described are similar to the picture one would have of a quarter or half moon. See Figure 15b. The clubhead is swung back on the outer perimeter and returns to the ball on the inner perimeter. The clubhead is not returned to the ball on the same path it described on the backswing. The direction of the backswing and the forward swing should be the same so that the player is retracing the direction of the backswing on the forward swing but not the path. Those players who attempt to retrace the path of the backswing will use a casting motion in order to accomplish it.

Photographs attempting to depict the shape of the swing have been published before, but due to the angle at which the camera was placed with regard to the swing plane, the shape of the swing was distorted and appeared much more elliptical than it is.

The illustrations shown in Figure 15 were taken so that the film plane was parallel to the plane of the swing—a driver was used. By placing the film plane parallel to the swing plane, the true shape of the golf swing can be seen. It much more closely resembles a circle than an ellipse.

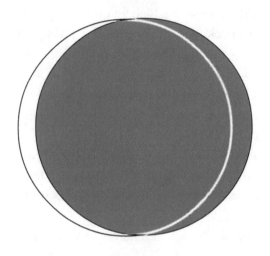

Figure 15a

The Role of the Back Foot

Which is the back foot? For right-handed players it is the right foot while for left-handed players it is the left foot. Very easy to remember.

Figure 15b

Figure 15c

The back foot is the key to keeping the body and the club's motion synchronized. It is a responsive movement. Test yourself by throwing a ball underhand down the fairway and you will clearly see how the back foot responds to the movement of the arm with which you throw the ball. Upon releasing the ball, check your back foot, the heel will be up so that the sole of your shoe is perpendicular to the ground. This is the same motion required in the golf swing.

For those of you who have back problems: If the back foot does not respond in the above manner, your back will be unduly twisted as the club proceeds into the follow through area. Everyone should have this type of back foot response, but for golfers who are prone to have back problems this is a must response. When the back foot responds as described above, the back does not get twisted and the player finishes erect with no strain on the back.

What happens to the swing when the back foot does not respond? The most flagrant error is that the shoulders will tend to be used to swing the club in the forward swing. This makes the club approach the ball with an outside to in pattern causing all sorts of different shots, none of them good. Mostly they will be pulled slices.

Even in the small shots, where the club reaches a horizontal level after impact, the back foot should react exactly the same way as it would in a full shot. If you are using a wedge to send the ball 30 yards, you should finish with the club pointing to the target, the back foot vertical to the ground, the body erect facing the target. You should be able to walk with the shot very comfortably with this type of movement. If the shot played is such that the club does not reach the horizontal level after impact, the back foot would have some response but would not end up vertical to the ground. The motion does not require that much movement.

I find that when players play small shots they tend to have a feeling that they should remain very still, so they plant their feet and keep them planted. It is difficult to swing the entire club forward when there is no response from the back foot.

The Swing Plane

What is meant by the swing plane? It is the inclination, the slant on which the golf club is swung with respect to the horizontal level of the ground. How is the plane of a player's swing determined? By drawing a line from the player's shoulders to the ball at the address position. How does the player determine the swing plane?

The plane is set the moment the player places the clubhead behind the golf ball. It is controlled by:

a. The length of the club being used. The shorter the club, the more upright the plane; the longer the club, the flatter the plane.

b. The height of the player. The taller the player the more up- right the plane; the shorter the player, the flatter the plane.

c. The posture of the player. The straighter the player stands at ad- dress, the more upright the plane; the more bend at the hips, the flatter the plane.

d. The distance of the player from the ball when addressing it. The closer the player is to the ball, the more upright the plane; the farther away from the ball, the flatter the plane.

e. The location of the ball. If the ball is below the player's feet, the more upright the plane; with the ball above the feet, the flatter the plane.

With the range of length in the clubs we use to play (14 according to the rules of golf), every golfer will use a minimum of 14 different planes.

This paragraph would make anyone attempting to learn to play golf shudder from the difficulty it seems to present. This feeling would be justified if you had to consciously control the plane of the different clubs. Fortunately, since the plane is set automatically when the clubhead is placed behind the ball at address, you do not have to be concerned with or be aware of it. The player does not control the plane consciously.

There is no need to think of it nor should there be any attempt to force the swing into a particular plane different from that set at the address position.

If the golf club is swung, it will remain on the plane in which it was set at the address position all by itself.

Upright And Flat Planes

Since the plane of the golf swing is the relationship between the inclination of the swing and the ground, a flat swing is one which has a more horizontal attitude while an upright swing is one which has a more vertical attitude.

It must be clearly understood that the words flat and upright are purely relative.

A swing that is considered upright for some players but fits them perfectly is really not upright for those players—it is their plane, but it may be very bad for some other players. Conversely, a swing that is considered flat but fits some players perfectly is not flat for them—it is their plane.

Thus, the words flat or upright must be used with respect to the same player. If a player makes a swing that is more upright or flatter than the plane should be, problems will arise because the normal plane has been altered. If a player has a swing that is more upright or flatter than that of some other players, it does not mean the plane is incorrect.

If a player, while learning, develops a swing that is in conflict with his or her normal plane, it will be more difficult for that player to perform a swing that is repetitive and easy to keep.

What happens to the swing plane as the golf club is swung? Once the club is swinging, it remains on the plane set at address if the player does not interfere. A swinging object never leaves its plane while in motion and its speed is maintained.

The pendulum of a grandfather clock never leaves its enclosure as long as it remains on its own and keeps on swinging, but if you touch it, the plane will change and it will have a wobbly motion. It will take some time for the true plane to be regained. The swinging of the pendulum will take care of it much better than if you try to get it swinging on the plane it should be on.

The plane of the backswing and the plane of the forward swing should be the same if one is to achieve perfection and be able to return the club to the address position with the greatest consistency.

The better the swinging motion is performed, the closer the player will be to having one plane, and thus the closer the player will come to perfection.

Weight Shift

A common theory claims that the weight should be shifted to the back foot in the backswing. I am convinced that the weight should not be transferred to the back foot in the backswing.

We are all looking for consistency in our games and we should swing the golf club so that it is easy to meet the golf ball with the face of the club at right angle to the target line. As mentioned before, the golf club is describing a circle when it is swung. Being a circle it must have a center. If we were describing a circle with a compass, the first thing we would do would be to set the center. If this center moves to different locations, it is impossible to return to the starting point.

The same thing happens in the golf swing. When the center is allowed to move to the right through a weight shift to the back foot, that center must be re-established prior to contacting the golf ball or square impact is impossible. You will observe some of our fine tournament players who do shift their center to the back foot and play well. But bear in mind that those players play every day and practice for hours every day. They have developed the timing and the extra move to achieve square impact. However, some of those same tournament players at times cannot find the timing to meet the ball properly and, especially with the driver, they become very inaccurate and miss more fairways than they should.

If the center is maintained, and the hands are placed on the club in a neutral position, the club can be returned to the exact address position from the end of the backswing and it will be square to the target line without any necessity to manipulate it to square. It is one less thing with which the player has to be concerned.

I contend that the weight should be maintained equally divided on the feet until after impact and then the centrifugal force will transfer the weight to the front foot.

Flexibility and Speed

Flexibility means lack of muscle tension. The more speed you desire, the more important flexibility becomes. If you were going to throw a ball as far as you could, you would not stiffen your arm. If you were going to kick a 50-yard field goal in football, you certainly would not stiffen your leg. If you wished to walk faster, you would not stiffen your legs.

For golf, tension is the player's greatest enemy, flexibility on the other hand is the player's greatest friend.

When the address position is taken, the arms should be in the same state as when they are hanging at the sides when standing erect, completely tension free. They must remain in this state while the swing is being performed. When the arms are completely tension free, that flexibility is transferred to the entire body. It allows the swing to be performed with a wonderful feeling of effortlessness.

What Does Swinging the Club at the Target Mean?

If an object is being propelled with another object in a certain direction, the direction of both objects must be the same.

A tennis player sending the tennis ball to the left corner of the left court swings the racquet in that direction. If a person is throwing a ball to another person, the arm necessarily moves in the direction of the person to whom the ball is being thrown.

It is such an obvious fact and yet golfers rarely think of it. If a player wishes the golf ball to fly to the target, the club being used must be swung in the direction of that target.

Players are always trying to get the ball to go someplace or not go someplace. The golf ball only reacts to what the club does, so again it's what we do with the golf club that is most important. If a player swings the golf club in the direction of the target, the ball is not going to be very far from it.

The easiest way to do this is through visualization. This means that while the swing is being performed, the player holds a mental image of the target and of the club swinging toward it. The player must have this mental image prior to starting the backswing and must hold it throughout the swing.

Needless to say, this assumes that the principles of the swinging motion previously discussed have been fulfilled.

The Follow-through

The follow-through is just the name given to that part of the swing from the ball to wherever the club stops after impact. When speaking of following through, it sounds as though the player is being given an order to do something to complete the swing after the ball is on its way.

I prefer to refer to the follow-through as the end of the swing. The follow-through or the end of the swing is not produced by the player, it is produced by the velocity with which the golf club has been swung, the player should have nothing to do with it. It is simply a result of producing the swing.

In order to have the speed of the swing produce the appropriate end of the swing, flexibility in the arms, freedom in the wrists, and complete body response is necessary, otherwise, the end of the swing will be cut short. The player will then be criticized for not following through. I would criticize the player for not allowing the club to reach the end of the swing on its own through the swing speed.

Swinging the Club and Playing through Application of the Proper Concept

A concept is an idea. With regard to the golf swing, it is the idea the player has of what should be done with the golf club in order to perform the golf swing. It is an image recalled by memory. It is the pattern of the swing calling for a plan of action. The concept, which we all should use when swinging a golf club, should be proven through practice and it must be supported by undeniable principles based on physics and geometry.

Once this concept has been determined, the player must use it in every swing whether it be on the practice tee or on the golf course while playing.

In 1942 while a member of the Northwestern University golf team I was a finalist in the NCAA Intercollegiate Championship. Upon my return home, my father asked me how I had played. I answered, "I played very well." Then he asked me if I knew what I was doing. I answered, "Yes I do." His last question was: "Does it work?" My answer was, "Yes, if I do it, it works." Then he said, "Son, if you know what you are doing and it works, spend the rest of your life perfecting it, and remember that if you should miss a shot, it simply means that you did not do what you were supposed to do, it does not mean that you did something wrong, so get back to what you should do." This meant—get back to your concept and perform it. No better advice could be given to anyone who wishes to maintain the game of golf at the highest level possible.

What my father was trying to do was to make me focus on the positive thing I had to do in order to be successful. As our friend and benefactor, Ernest Jones, said to my father many times in my presence: There is nothing wrong if you do it right.

This attitude eliminates the tendency that we all have to try to correct something that in our mind produced the missed shot. Since many things can cause a missed shot, the more we attempt to make a correction, the further away we get from our concept—the one that produces the desired results for us.

I have thanked my father so many times for this advice—which made it possible for me to forget my bad shots and build on the mental image of only my good swings. This in turn makes my desire to produce my concept so much stronger. Nothing else matters.

Everyone can build on this advice. I will repeat the concept again:

I will swing the clubhead with my hands in the backswing so my club ends over my shoulder, and I will then swing the entire club with my arms in one uninterrupted motion in the direction of my target to the end of my swing, allowing my body to respond to the swing.

Remember and believe that this concept never produces a bad shot. You don't have to worry about anything else.

Not only is this concept composed of easily understood principles, but these principles can readily be converted into a simple, smooth, constant and effective movement to propel the golf ball.

If a golf swing is simple, smooth and constant, it will be most effective, and a pleasure to experience.

I invite you all, amateurs and professionals alike, to try it. I am sure you will like it, and best of all, you will play better golf.

Part III

Cause and Effect
and Corrections

Chapter 5

Common Problems

Throughout this book I advocate that the swinging motion produced with a golf club is a very simple thing and yet in this section I present a very profound analysis of what the ball does, why it does it, and how to change it. This does not make the swing complicated.

As you read the analyses of common ball flight patterns that follow, be objective and notice the common sense in reasoning what the ball does. There is no mystery in what the ball does. It is very logical and it always reverts back to what the player does or does not do with the golf club. To me as a player, as well as an instructor, it is essential to know and understand the causes of the various ball flight patterns. To the reader it should be just as important.

It takes a very short time to change an undesirable ball flight to a desirable one, but you have to determine the cause of the ball flight you wish to change. The pages that follow supply you with the knowledge you need to do this analysis and make the necessary correction.

What is cause and effect? It is something that happens (the effect) and that which makes it happen (the cause). Lack of understanding of cause and effect is one of the greatest contributors to golfers' confusion regarding the golf swing and the flight of the golf ball.

The effects on the flight of the golf ball are very specific, but similar effects can have very different causes. And this is where the average golfer does a great deal of damage to his or her swing and to that of others to whom well-meaning help is given. So many times players do exactly what they are trying to correct because of lack of knowledge and understanding of cause and effect. When the attempted corrections do not work or help the problem, the dilemma becomes even more distressing.

The difficulty is that people seldom feel that study is necessary to become a golfer. Somehow, just putting a golf club in someone's hand and wielding it is good enough. Unfortunately, to become a good player it isn't enough. Someone trying to play chess has to go through a learning process—what the moves are, why and when to make them. And this learning process isn't just a matter of a few minutes, a day, a week, or a month. Study and understanding are essential to become a good golfer, especially understanding the basic principles and concepts of physics. Every motion (cause) produced with our body or our club and every thought (cause) or change of thought have certain reactions (effects), and to be successful we should know what they are.

The principles and concepts are very simple—it's just a matter of learning their proper application.

If understanding cause and effect is so important to the amateur player, imagine how important it is to a professional who is trying to teach the golf swing and make swing corrections. Without this understanding it is impossible to give anyone lasting and satisfying help.

Note for Left-Handed Players: *In the following discussion, hand placement, ball placement, and ball flight must be reversed for left-handed players.*

Slicing

1.   Incorrect Positioning of the Left Hand On the Golf Club

If the left hand is positioned on the club so that the **V** formed by the thumb and the index finger points to the left of the center of the body, it will:

    a.   Increase the loft of the clubface.

    b.   Cause the clubface to be aiming to the right at impact.

    c.   Cause the golf ball to spin clockwise, thus producing a slice.

    d.   Cause the shots to be quite high.

    e.   Cause the shots to be very short in distance.

In view of these results, a shot made with the left hand in this position will start to the right of the target. It will be very high and will slice. The direction error will be very great because the ball starts to the right and then goes farther to the right because of the clockwise spin.

Correction

Move your left hand to the right until the **V** points to the center of your body. It will then be right on top of the center line of the shaft of the club pointing to the center of your body.

Principle

The hands should be naturally balanced when holding the golf club. What does naturally balanced mean? Consider these two balance principles for the hands:

- Balance in relation to each other. The palms of the hands face each other.

- Balance in relation to the target line. The palm of the right hand should be facing down the fairway, and a perpendicular line drawn from it will be parallel to the target line. The palm of the left hand will oppose it.

Get your hands balanced on the golf club.

---

2.   Incorrect Positioning of Right Hand On the Golf Club

If the right hand is positioned on the golf club so that the **V** formed by the thumb and the index finger points to the left of the center of the body, it will:

a. Increase the loft of the clubface

b. Cause the clubface to be aiming to the right at impact.

c. Cause the golf ball to spin clockwise, thus producing a slice.

d. Cause the shots to be quite high.

e. Cause the shots to be very short in distance.

In view of these results, a shot made with the right hand in this position will start to the right of the target, it will be very high and will slice. The direction error will be very great because the ball starts to the right and then goes farther to the right because of the clockwise spin.

Correction

Move your right hand to the right until the **V** points to the center of your body. It will then be right on top of the center line of the shaft of the golf club.

Principle

Same as principle in Section 1.

Get your hands balanced on the golf club.

---

3. *Taking the Clubhead Back Outside of the Target Line*

Causes

1. Using a tilting action with the shoulders to start the backswing, but using the hands to swing the club back.

2. Addressing the golf ball so that the shoulder line is not on the same plane as the target line and the direction of the shoulder plane is to the left, normally referred to as open.

3. Using the left arm to push the club back to start the backswing.

4. Keeping the arms and shoulders too rigid causing a backswing as described in #1 above.

5. Fear of slicing: Starting the backswing on the outside so that the club can be swung to the left in an effort to prevent the slice.

6. Holding the body too still, not responsive to the club's motion.

7. Lack of awareness of the target.

8. Placing the ball too far toward the front foot.

Effect

When the clubhead is taken back on the outside of the target line, the clubhead will cut across the target line toward the left in the forward swing causing:

    a.   The ball to start to the left of the target line.

    b.   The clubhead to impart a clockwise spin to the ball which will make it slice.

    c.   The shot to be lower than normal.

    d.   The ball to be contacted off center on the clubface.

Correction

The correction depends on the cause of the problem and will not be the same for every player.

To correct #1, #3, and #4: Swing the clubhead with your hands in one motion to the end of your backswing.

To correct #2: Address the ball with a very relaxed attitude to eliminate tension, and the clubface should be at a right angle to the target line. The body should be facing the clubface squarely, meaning that the shoulder line, if the shoulders were level, would be parallel to the target line. Since the shoulders are not level at the address position, they cannot be parallel to the target line but must be on the same plane. This relaxed attitude will also be most helpful in correcting #4.

To correct #5: You have to realize that slicing cannot be corrected by trying to correct the ball flight. The principle stated below must be applied.

To correct #6: You must be in a relaxed state and when the motion of the club starts, your body simply responds to that motion and goes along with it so that there is complete synchronization between body and club motions.

To correct #8: Move the ball and the club toward the back foot until the clubhead is in the center of the stance, then the shoulders will be on the same plane as the target line.

Principle

The clubhead must be swung back from the ball in a circular pattern. When the club is swinging, the shaft reaches a horizontal level at five different locations in the swing.

1. Halfway in the backswing.
2. At the end of the backswing if the player is making a full swing.
3. Halfway between the end of the backswing, moving toward the ball in the forward swing.
4. Past the ball after impact.
5. When the club approaches the end of the swing, in fuller swings only.

At every one of these horizontal locations, the shaft of the golf club should be parallel to the target line.

4. Clubhead Moved Straight Back From the Ball In the Backswing

The causes and effects of moving the clubhead straight back from the ball in the backswing are the same as you read in Section 3. The matter of degree is the only difference, the degree being much less when the club moves straight back instead of outside the target line.

Effect

See Section 3—Swinging the clubhead outside of the target line.

Correction

See section 3.

5. Left Wrist Too Firm Approaching the Ball in the Forward Swing

Causes

1. Trying to keep the ball from hooking.

2. Trying to have the hands ahead of the clubhead at impact.

3. Exerting a pulling action with the left arm in order to swing the club forward.

Effect

a. At the moment of impact all three causes above will cause the clubhead to be out of square and aiming to the right.

b. This type of contact of the clubhead with the ball will cause the ball to spin clockwise, producing a slice.

c. Ball will start straight toward the target, then curve to the right.

d. Height of the shots will be quite normal.

Explanation

The clubhead is out of square when it aims to the right or left of the target but retains its normal loft.

The clubhead is open when it aims to the right and its loft is increased.

Correction

To correct #1: No effort should be made to prevent any type of ball flight. You should always try to send the ball straight to the target.

To correct #2: You should understand that both ends of the club must be in the same position at impact as they were at the address position.

To correct #3: The club has to be swung, not pulled or pushed. The forces used to pull or push have a straight line attitude, meaning that when an object is pulled or pushed, the direction of the force used is straight not circular. A golf swing is a circular motion, it has no straight lines anywhere.

6. Using the Shoulders To Start the Forward Swing

Causes

1. Fear of slicing will make a player spin to the left with the shoulders in an effort to keep the ball from slicing.

2. Using the shoulders in an effort to increase distance.

3. Keeping the lower part of the body (from the waist down) unresponsive to the swinging motion.

4. Becoming too rigid in the arms and shoulders, thus eliminating the freedom that should exist in the upper torso.

5. Not realizing that the forward swing is the responsibility of the arms—not other parts of the body.

Effect

In all of the above, the direction of the swing is changed to the left, causing the club to approach the ball from the outside. It will be cutting across the target line to the left. The result will be the same as in Section 3.

a.   The ball will start to the left of the target line.

b.   The clubhead will impart a clockwise spin to the ball, making it slice.

c.   The shots will tend to be lower than normal.

d.   Ball contact will be off center on the face of the club. It could be on the toe or on the heel depending on what the player does with the club.

Correction

The responsibility for the forward swing must be returned to the arms, both arms. They must swing the entire club from the end of the backswing to the end of the swing in one uninterrupted motion in the direction of the target, allowing the right heel to rise as the forward swing progresses. The shoulders will then respond to the swinging motion. This responsive attitude will guarantee that the shoulders move properly and will be synchronized with the golf club.

If the player uses the arms to swing the club from the end of the backswing to the finish of the swing, the shoulders will not interfere.

---

7. Keeping The Left Arm Straight Or Rigid

The left arm should be permitted to remain as extended as possible but without any tension. The arm movement in the backswing is a duplicate but opposite from that of the forward swing.

In the backswing: The right arm bends.
The left arm extends.

In the forward swing: The right arm extends.
The left arm bends.

If a player keeps the right arm as straight in the backswing as players are led to believe the left should be, the club could never swing around the body.

The same thing would happen in the forward swing—if the left arm is kept as straight as the right, the club could never swing around the body.

Players who make a conscious effort to keep the left arm straight in the backswing, keep it straight through rigidity, the greatest enemy of any golf swing.

Keeping the left arm straight in this manner causes the face of the club to open as it reaches the ball. When a ball is struck with an open face:

1. It will start to the right of the target line.

2. It will go very high.

3. It will be spinning clockwise, therefore slicing.

4. It will not go very far.

Shots played with this firmness in the left arm will be very short for two reasons. First, an open face directs the golf ball upward not forward. Second, in order to develop velocity there has to be flexibility and freedom in every part that is instrumental in swinging the club. With the left arm rigid this flexibility and freedom do not exist.

If a person wanted to walk faster, would he stiffen his legs? Certainly not.

8. *Keeping Or Increasing the Weight on the Back Foot In the Forward Swing*

Causes

1. Fear of slicing.

2. Trying to get under the golf ball.

3. Rigidity in the legs.

4. Trying to get the right shoulder under in the forward swing.

5. Keeping the head down too long.

6. Not allowing the right heel to rise as a response in the forward swing.

Effect

All six causes above will force the clubhead to be open at impact.

Correction

To correct #1: You must set in your mind that your purpose is to send the ball straight to the target, not to keep it from going to the right or left.

To correct #2: You should attempt to send the ball on a straight line to the target, not up to the sky. The height of every shot is determined primarily by the loft of the club being used. Let the loft of the clubhead raise the golf ball—that is not the player's responsibility. The player's responsibility is to send the ball forward towards the target.

To correct #3: Your legs should be very supple and responsive. Bracing them will impede your swing and the response of your body to the swing. Direction and distance will be affected.

To correct #4: Allow your shoulders, right and left, to respond to the swinging motion. There should be no effort on your part to influence how they move. If they respond, they will move correctly.

To correct #5: Instead of trying to keep your head down, keep your eyes on the ball, as you would in any other sport.

To correct #6: The right heel is instrumental in developing good synchronization between your body movement and the club's swinging motion. Permit or allow your right heel to rise as the forward swing progresses.

9. Opening the Clubhead In the Forward Swing

Concern with getting the ball into the air and trying to scoop it.

Effect

This problem can produce opposite ball reactions depending upon the degree to which the clubhead is opened. Normally, the ball will:

a. Start to the right of the target.

b. Go very high.

c. Have a clockwise spin causing the ball to slice.

d. Not have much distance.

If this problem is exaggerated, the ball will be struck by the sole line of the clubhead in an upward direction causing it to be topped and to roll along the ground.

Correction

You must return the clubhead to the ball so that at the moment of impact the clubface is at a right angle to the target line. Visualize this while the swing is in progress. After contact, when the club reaches a horizontal level after impact, the shaft of the club should be parallel to the target line and the toe of the clubhead should be pointing to the sky

10. Gripping The Golf Club With The Face Open
Effect

    a.   Ball will start to the right of the target

    b.   Trajectory of the shot will be very high.

    c.   Ball will have a clockwise spin causing it to slice.

    d.   Distance will be very short.

Correction

You must learn to perceive a right angle between the target line and the clubface at the address position.

Procedure

- Place a club on the ground pointing to the target and then place the face of the club to be swung at a right angle to the shaft of the club on the ground representing the target line.

- Be very observant when taking the grip and watch the clubface to be sure that it does not change during the process of gripping the club.

- Without releasing the grip, move away from the club on the ground and repeat the procedure over and over again to train the eyes to accomplish the right angle alignment at address.

II. Club Approaching the Ball in the Forward Swing in a Direction that Is Too Far from the Inside and with a Stiff Left Arm

Cause

Believing the club should be swung inside out with a straight left arm.

Effect

Swinging the club forward from an exaggerated inside out direction will make the club swing to the right of the target. This, coupled with a stiff left arm at impact, will not only make the club go to the right, but will also open the clubface. The ball will be directed way right of the target and in addition the spin caused by the open clubface will cause the ball to slice, thereby going even farther to the right.

Correction

1. Release the stiffness of your left arm so it is flexible and supple at the address position. It must be kept that way while swinging.

2. Swing the club away from the ball in a circular motion so that when the club reaches the halfway point in the backswing and it is horizontal, the shaft is parallel to the target line with the toe of the clubhead pointing to the sky.

   If you swing the club back too far to the inside, when it reaches the horizontal level halfway to the end of the backswing, it will not be parallel to the target line, it will point to the right.

3. In the forward swing, swing the club so that when it reaches the halfway point to the ball, it is again parallel to the target line.

12. Swinging the Clubhead Back With the Left Hand Only (Left-Hand Dominance)

When the clubhead is swung back with just the left hand, the left hand will use the right wrist as a pivoting point and will work around it.

This will make the clubhead rotate so that when the club reaches the horizontal level, halfway in the backswing, the face of the club will be facing upward toward the sky, and the shaft of the club will be pointing to the right of the target. This position of the club is normally referred to as being laid off. When the club is in this laid off position in the backswing, it forces the clubhead to return to the ball with the face open, especially if the left arm is rigid, which will cause:

a.   The ball to start to the right of the target.

b.   The shot to be much higher than normal.

c.   The ball to have a clockwise spin, causing it to slice.

d.   The distance to be very poor.

Correction

You must swing the clubhead back with both the right and left hands. Your right hand must be involved in the backswing to the same degree as your left. By using both hands, you can keep the golf club on the proper plane.

Principle

Since your hands are linked together through the interlocking or overlapping grips, or placed very close together in the ten finger grip, they must work as a unit. Each hand has a very different motion depending on the direction in which they are moving, but when used in conjunction with each other they act with a balanced attitude. This means that your hands will not rotate the clubhead at any point in the backswing, and your ability to return the clubhead to the ball in a square position to the target line is enhanced 100%.

Important Warning: *When the club is laid off it does not mean that it is too far to the inside. You should not attempt to correct this problem by trying to make the swing more upright, or by trying to change the direction in which the club is swung back.*

---

13. *Tilting the Shoulders At the Start of the Forward Swing*
Causes

1. Using the shoulders in an effort to get under the ball in order to lift it.

2. Believing that an attempt should be made to get the shoulder under the chin in the forward swing. This happens normally without trying.

Effect

  a. Clubhead will reach the ball with an open face.

  b. The golf ball will start to the right of the target.

  c. The trajectory will be very high.

  d. Distance will be short.

  e. Player will finish the swing with his back very arched, leaning backward. This can cause severe back problems.

  f. Player will be unable to finish with the weight on the forward foot.

  g. Ball will have a clockwise spin, causing it to slice.

Correction

The responsibility for the forward swing must be given to your arms since they must swing the club from the end of the backswing to the finish of the swing.

  The direction of the swing must be toward the target, but when the shoulders are tilted, the direction of the club as it is swinging is upward and not toward the target.

14. *Restricting the Backswing Size by Reducing the Body's Response*
Causes

1. Thinking that the backswing is too long.

2. Too much rigidity in arms and wrists.

Effect

When the backswing is restricted by reducing the body response, which in turn reduces the shoulder turn, the forward swing will be started with the shoulders being overturned at the beginning of the forward swing. This will result in:

a. The club being forced to approach the golf ball from a line crossing the target line to the left (outside in).

b. The center of the swing moving to the left before impact.

c. The ball starting out to the left of the target.

d. The ball developing a clockwise spin causing it to slice.

e. The trajectory of the shot being lowered considerably.

f. Distance being very poor.

If this problem is exaggerated, it could result in topping the ball.

Correction

To correct #1: You should make no effort to decrease your backswing by restricting your body response. The size of the backswing should be an instinctive reaction based on the distance the ball is to be sent. In full shots, the size of the backswing depends mostly on the player's flexibility, and this differs from player to player.

To correct #2: At all times, flexibility and freedom are essential for good performance, consistency, and speed. You must maintain an attitude of ease in the body and arms—any rigidity translates into failure.

Whether the swing is short or long, you must remain 100% synchronized and unified with the club's motion. If you wish to play with a shorter swing, you must allow your body to respond naturally to the shorter swing. The swing cannot be shortened by restricting your body motion and still have shots of good quality.

When swinging the club back, the clubhead and the shoulders must start together and must stay together until the backswing is completed.

15. Placement of Golf Ball Too Far Toward the Forward Foot at Address

Effect

  a. Player will tend to swing the club back on the outside.

  b. The shoulders will be lined up too far to the left of the target.

  c. Ball will start to the left of the target.

  d. Ball will have a clockwise spin, which will make it slice.

  e. Trajectory of the shot will tend to be quite normal.

Correction

To be in perfect balance at the address position, place the clubhead so that it is in the center of the stance. The ball will be slightly to the left next to the clubhead. With the clubhead placed in the center, your shoulders will align themselves perfectly and automatically.

Principle

Balance is very important in a golf swing—balance in relation to your weight and balance of your body in relation to the target line. The only way to achieve body balance easily and correctly at the address position is to have the clubhead in the center of your stance.

The center of your stance is the point where a vertical line from the midpoint between your shoulders touches the ground. Do not try to find the center of your stance by determining the midpoint of the distance between the toes of your shoes.

When the ball position is varied, the direction of the backswing changes. If it is moved too far toward the front foot, you will start the club toward the outside of the target line. If the ball is placed too far toward the back foot, you will start the club too far to the inside.

Placing the clubhead in the center of the stance will make all swings more consistent.

Consistency in a golf swing is essential in order to play well, score well, and have confidence in one's swing and game.

---

16. Placement of Golf Ball Too Far Toward the Back Foot at Address

Effect

    a.   Player will tend to swing the club too far inside.

    b.   Clubface will be out of square.

    c.   Ball will start to the right of the target.

    d.   Ball will have a clockwise spin, which will make it slice.

    e.   Trajectory of the shot will tend to be lower than normal.

Correction and Principle

Same as for Section #15

17. Driving with the Legs on the Forward Swing

Effect

Using the legs in the forward swing will curve the body so that it tilts backward. This will open the clubface so that:

    a.   The club's direction will be upward toward the sky instead of toward the target.

    b.   The ball will start to the right of the target.

    c.   Trajectory of the shot will be higher than normal.

    d.   Distance will be very poor.

    e.   Ball will have a clockwise spin, causing it to slice.

Correction

Responsibility for swinging the club forward should rest with your arms not your legs. Your legs should respond to the motion of the club but should not be involved in influencing the swing.

Test

- Swing the club to the end of the backswing and stop. Use your legs but have no arm motion. The club does not move very much.

- Swing the club to the end of the backswing and stop. Use your arms and simply allow your legs to respond naturally. The club will fly to the finish.

Your legs have no connection to the club, the arms do.

18. Turning the Hips to Get Them Out of the Way on the Forward Swing

Effect

    a.   Turning the hips will make the entire body spin to the left.

    b.   The club is forced to the outside of the target line.

    c.   Ball will start to the left of the target.

    d.   Clubface will be out of square.

    e.   This action will give the ball greater clockwise spin, thus producing a greater slice.

    f.   Trajectory of the shot will tend to be lower.

    g.   Distance will be very poor.

Correction

Responsibility for the forward swing must be returned to your arms, and your hips must be allowed to respond to the swinging motion.

Use the same test as in Section 17, but use your hips instead of your legs.

19. *Pushing off Right Foot to Start the Forward Swing*
Effect

    a. Weight transfers to front foot too soon.

    b. Finish of the swing is quite short.

    c. Clubhead reaches the ball out of square.

    d. Balance is poor at the end of the swing.

    e. Ball starts to the right of the target.

    f. Trajectory of the shot is quite low.

    g. Distance is poor.

    h. Ball will have a clockwise spin, causing it to slice.

    i. At impact, the center of the swing is past the golf ball.

Correction

When addressing the golf ball, your weight should be equally distributed on each foot. It must remain equally distributed until impact, at which time it transfers to the front foot because of the pulling action of the club caused by the velocity with which it is being swung. Transferring the weight prematurely makes it impossible to return the clubface to the ball at a right angle to the target line.

The center of the swing must remain the center until the ball is struck. The golf swing is circular, and without a center the club cannot return to the point of departure and be in the exact position at impact as it was at the address position without a great deal of manipulation.

Hooking

I. *Incorrect Position of the Left Hand*

If the left hand is placed on the golf club so that the **V** formed by the thumb and index finger points to the right of the center of the body, the following will be the result:

Effect

a. When the club is swung, the centrifugal force created by the motion will tend to close the clubhead.

b. When the closed face contacts the ball, it will impart a counter-clockwise spin to the ball producing a hooked shot.

c. The closed face will decrease the loft of the clubface so the shots will be lower than normal.

d. Distance will be shortened with regards to carry, although the ball will have greater roll.

With this clubhead position, the ball will have a tendency to start to the left, and adding the ball spin to this, the directional error will be very great.

Correction

Turn the hand to the left until the **V** formed by the thumb and the index finger points to the center of the body. It will be on the top of the shaft.

Principle

See Section 1 under Slicing, p.72.

2.   *Incorrect Position of the Right Hand*

If your right hand is placed on the golf club so that the **V** formed by your thumb and index finger points to the right of the center of the body, the following will be the result:

Effect

    a. When the club is swung, the centrifugal force created by the motion will tend to close the clubface.

    b. When the closed clubface contacts the ball, it will impart a counterclockwise spin to the ball, producing a hooked shot.

    c. The closed face will decrease the loft of the club, so the shots will be lower than normal.

    d. Distance will be shortened with regards to the carry, although the ball will have greater roll.

With this clubhead position, the ball will have a tendency to start to the left of the target, and adding the ball spin to this, the directional error will be very great.

Correction

Turn your hand to the left until the **V** formed by your thumb and index finger points to the center of the body. It will be on the top of the shaft.

Principle

See Section 1 under Slicing, p.72.

3.   *Incorrect Position of Both Hands*

If both hands are placed on the club so each **V** points to the right of the center of the body, the effects listed in Section 1 and 2 will be the same, but because both hands are out of balance, these effects will be much greater.

Correction

Both hands must be turned to the left until each **V** points to the center of the body. They will then be on the top of the shaft and in line with each other.

Principle

See Section 1 under Slicing, p.72.

4. Gripping the Club With the Face Closed

If both hands are placed on the club in a balanced position, both in relation to each other and to the target line, but the clubface is closed, the following will result:

Effect

    a. When the closed clubface contacts the ball, it will impart a counterclockwise spin to the ball producing a hooked shot.

    b. The closed clubface will decrease the loft so the shots will be lower than normal.

    c. Distance will be shortened with regards to carry, although the ball will have greater roll.

With this clubface position, the ball will have a tendency to start to the left of the target, and adding the ball spin to this, the directional error will be very great.

Correction

You must learn to perceive a right angle between the target line and the clubface when addressing the golf ball.

Procedure

Refer to Procedure in Section 10 under Slicing, p.81.

5. Club Placed Too Far Toward the Tips of the Fingers of the Left Hand

When the club is placed too far out in the fingertips, when gripping pressure is applied, as the fingers close, they rotate the golf club and therefore close the clubface.

Effect

a.   Ball will start to the left of the target.

b.   Trajectory of the shot will be lower than normal.

c.   The clubface will impart a counterclockwise spin to the golf ball, causing it to curve to the left.

d.   Distance of carry will be diminished, but the ball will have greater roll.

Correction

Once you place your left hand on the club, the fingers should be wrapped around the shaft so that all parts of the fingers are in contact with the club. Increasing the pressure of the grip should not rotate the club.

6. Using the Shoulders to Start the Forward Swing and Closing the Clubface with the Hands at Impact

Effect

a.   Because the shoulders are involved, the ball will be pulled much more than when just the clubface meets the ball in a closed position.

b.   The closed clubface imparts a counterclockwise spin to the ball, causing it to curve to the left.

c.   The ball will fly lower than normal.

d.   The ball will have a short carry and a great deal of roll.

Correction

The responsibility for the forward swing must be returned to your arms, both arms. Your arms must swing the entire club from the end of the backswing to the end of the swing in one uninterrupted motion in the direction of the target. Your shoulders will then respond to the swinging motion. This responsive attitude will guarantee that your shoulders move properly and are synchronized with the golf club's motion.

The arms keep the hands from being used as the clubhead approaches the golf ball.

When the arms are used to swing the entire golf club from the end of the backswing to the finish of the swing, the shoulders and the hands will not interfere.

---

7. Closing the Clubhead as it Is Started Back, and Keeping It Closed during the Entire Swing

Cause

1. Attempting to keep the clubface square with the target line in the backswing.

2. Using the left hand (right hand for left-handed players) to start the backswing with an under curling action. This means rotating the left hand so that the palm turns to face the sky.

3. Using the arms with rigidity to make the backswing.

Effect

   a.   Ball will start left of target and curve to the left.

   b.   Ball will fly lower than normal.

   c.   The ball will have a short carry and lots of roll.

Correction

Swing the clubhead back from the ball with your hands, keeping your arms very flexible so that when the shaft reaches the first horizontal position, halfway in the backswing, it is parallel to the target line with the toe of the clubhead pointing to the sky.

8. *Swinging the Club Back Too Far Inside and Swinging Forward Inside Out With a Rolling (Closing) Action of the Clubhead By the Hands*

Cause

The player feels that the club should be swung with an inside out direction so that is the direction in which the club is swung back. However, this direction gives the player the sensation that the ball is going to be sent to the right and makes the player use his or her hands to change the direction of the ball, with the hope that it can be sent to the target. This hand action also gives the player the feeling of power even though the opposite is true. The swinging motion has greater speed.

Effect

    a.   The ball will start to the right of the target and then curve to the left.

    b.   The height of the shot will have great variation depending:

- On the person's swing.
- The degree of hand rotation.

Correction

You have to change your understanding of the golf swing. If you want to send the ball straight to the target, the club cannot be swung inside out. The geometric principle behind this is stated below. The second part of the correction is that your hands must remain passive as your arms fulfill their responsibility in the forward swing.

Principle

The geometric principle that applies to the golf swing is as follows: We have established that the golf swing is a circle, and a circle is always on a plane. All the horizontal chords of a circle are parallel to each other as well as parallel to the horizontal tangents. The target line is a horizontal tangent. When the club is swinging and it reaches a horizontal position anywhere in the swing, the shaft must be parallel to the target line.

If a club is swung inside out or outside in, that club does not fulfill the stated geometric principle. In an inside out swing, the club shaft points to the right at the horizontal levels at the midpoints of the swing, thereby cutting through the plane.

9. Swinging the Club Correctly in the Backswing but Returning It Too Far from the Inside on the Forward Swing with a Rolling Action of the Clubhead as It Approaches the Ball

Cause

1. Feeling that the club should be swung inside out in the forward swing even though the swing was made correctly in the backswing. Because the player senses that the ball will go to the right, an attempt is made to change the direction of the shot by using the hands and rotating the clubhead to the left.

2. Trying to get the right elbow (left elbow for left-handed players) close to the body as the forward swing is started.

Effect

Because the player senses that the ball will go to the right, he or she attempts to change the direction of the shot by using the hands and rotating the clubhead to the left. This creates a right to left hook.

The elbow does not get close to the body in the forward swing. It is the body turn that produces the closeness between the elbow or arm and the body. When the player makes an effort to make the elbow get close to the body, the direction of the swing is changed by dropping the club too far to the inside and flattening the plane.

Correction

Swing the golf club from the end of the backswing in a forward direction (toward the target) not inside out. Swing with your arms, and when the club reaches a horizontal level, the shaft of the club should be parallel to the target line.

By swinging the golf club with your arms and allowing your body to respond to the swinging motion, your elbow and your body will be very close as the forward swing is produced. There is no need to force this closeness to happen.

10. Tilting the Shoulders to Start the Backswing in an Effort to Keep the Left Shoulder Under the Chin

Effect

a. The clubhead gets closed as the player swings the club away from the ball. The hands are not involved in the start of the backswing.

b. The ball will start to the left of the target.

c. The closed clubhead will give the ball a counterclockwise spin, which will make it curve left.

Correction

You must swing the clubhead back with your hands, not your shoulders. No effort should be made to force your left shoulder under your chin. If your body is as responsive as it should be, your shoulder response will be adequate and proper.

II. **Left-Hand Dominance In the Backswing**

Definition

Left-hand dominance means that the left hand is used exclusively to swing the clubhead away from the ball in the backswing.

Effect

a. The plane of the swing is flattened.

b. The club's shaft will not be parallel to the target line when it reaches the horizontal level halfway in the backswing, it will point to the right.

c. The player will react on the forward swing with a strong closing rotation of the clubhead in an attempt to get the face square to the target line. However, this reaction is usually so strong that the ball will be struck with a closed face, causing it to curve left.

d. If in addition to the left-hand dominance problem the player maintains the left arm in a rigid state, the shot will be extremely high, very short in distance, and the direction will be very far to the right.

Correction

You must swing the clubhead back with both hands. Your right hand must be involved in the backswing to the same degree as the left.

Warning: *Using the right hand does not mean using the right arm to swing the club back.*

---

12. Keeping the Clubface Square To the Target Line as the Club Is Swung Back From the Ball In the Backswing

Effect

a.   The clubhead will get closed very soon.

b.   The ball will start to the left of the target and curve left.

c.   Shots will tend to be lower.

Correction

Swing the clubhead so that when the club reaches the first horizontal position halfway in the backswing, the shaft is parallel to the target line and the toe of the club points to the sky.

13. Swinging the Club In the Proper Direction in Both Backswing and Forward Swing, but the Hands Roll the Clubhead as It Nears the Ball

Effect

The golf ball will start straight to the target but then will curve left.

Correction

The responsibility for the forward swing must be returned to your arms, both arms.

Your arms must swing the entire club from the end of the backswing to the finish of the swing in one uninterrupted motion in the direction of the target.

If the arms fulfill their responsibility of swinging the entire club from the end of the backswing to the finish of the swing, the hands will not be involved.

---

14. Trying To Stay Behind the Ball On the Forward Swing

Effect

a. The player tends to lean back to stay behind the ball.

b. Proper body response is not possible.

c. The player can move the club too much inside out.

d. The ball will tend to fly higher than normal because as the player leans backward the club is swung more upward. If this is exaggerated, topping could be the result.

e. The clubhead will have a tendency to close. With this tendency and the club swinging upward, very severe hooks are the result.

f. If, however the player adds a firm left arm to his idea of staying behind the ball, huge high slices can be the result.

Correction

You should remain in the same balanced attitude while swinging as at address. The center of your swing should remain the center, and keeping your weight equally divided on the feet will accomplish this. The weight will then transfer to your front foot because of the pull of the club in the direction of the target. By trying to stay behind the ball you destroy the synchronization between the body's and the club's motion. Staying behind the ball prevents proper shifting of the weight on the forward swing.

Casting

Casting is the action of throwing the clubhead toward the golf ball at any point in the forward swing, although most golfers tend to cast at the beginning of the forward swing.

Cause

Thrusting the clubhead at the ball with the intent of using it to strike the golf ball or in an effort to create a very fast clubhead speed.

Effect

Casting is the use of one hand against the other. The right hand is the one that originates this type of problem in a right-handed player, the left in a left-handed player. The use of the right or left hand as the case may be causes the grip pressure in that hand to increase. The stronger the cast, the greater the pressure increase.

Casting can also be produced by the use of the forearm (right for right-handed players and left for left-handed players) as the player starts the forward swing. The result is just the same as when the right hand is used). The intent is still the same, i.e., to get the clubhead back to the ball or to generate more clubhead speed.

Correction

There are several ways to correct this problem. First, you must have the proper mental picture of what a swing looks like.

Anyone who visualizes the backswing and the return to the golf ball as having the same path will always use a casting motion.

The picture of that part of the swing is like a half moon. In the correct swing, the club swings back from the ball to the end of the back-swing on the outer perimeter but returns to the ball on the inner perimeter. This does not mean that the forward part of the swing is inside of the backswing. They should both be on the same plane. Just as one can draw it on a piece of paper.

Next, do one of the following:

a.   Do not allow the pressure in your right hand to increase anywhere in the forward swing.

b.   Use your arms and let them be responsible for the forward swing.

c.   Keep your hands passive in the forward swing.

By applying any one of the above points a, b, or c, casting is not possible. You must determine which one of a, or b, or c works best for you. Some players need only one of the three, other players may be able to handle only two of them, while others can handle all three. Just applying one of the three can be sufficient.

If you use "a", your arms will take over, the pressure will not increase, and your hands will remain passive.

If you use "b", your hands will remain passive, and by remaining passive the pressure will not increase.

If you use "c", your arms must take over and the pressure will not increase. Singly or in combination with each other, a, b, and c will bring good results.

Note: *Not allowing the pressure in the grip to increase does not mean that the grip should be lightened. It simply means that as far as the player is concerned, the pressure stays as constant as possible in the player's normal grip.*

Topping the Ball

Practically all golfers who top the ball feel they are looking up or peeking. So they concentrate very hard on keeping their head down or staying down and they keep on topping the ball anyway.

Causes

1. Attempting to get the ball into the air, and doing it with all clubs.

   a. Using the hands as the clubhead reaches the ball. The hands open the clubface to get the ball up, which makes the bottom of the club contact the ball instead of making contact with the surface of the clubface.

   b. Tipping the swing so the club is moving upward toward the sky in the forward swing, keeping the weight of the body on the back foot. This places the lowest point of the arc too far behind the ball. After the club reaches the lowest point of the arc, it starts to rise and it will be too high by the time it reaches the ball. Topping is the result.

2. Holding the body too still (planted and unresponsive) on the forward swing, producing the same result as in #1a above.

3. Trying to get the club under the ball, which will have the same effect as #1b above. Since the ground is under the ball, it is not possible to get under the ball.

4. Exerting a pulling action with the left arm as the club approaches the ball, which creates rigidity in the left wrist causing the clubhead to approach the golf ball too high.

5. A sudden change in acceleration with the arms as the clubhead approaches the golf ball, producing the same result as in #4.

6. Rigidity in the wrists in the forward swing, with the same results as in #4 and #5.

7. Standing too far from the ball.

8. Making an effort to shift the weight to the front foot prematurely, which causes the center of the swing to be ahead of the golf ball. The lowest point of the arc is too far to the target side of the golf ball so the clubhead is too high at impact.

9. Starting the forward swing with the shoulders, which produces the same result as in #8.

10. Placing the golf ball too far toward the back foot at address. The clubhead reaches the ball too early and too high on the arc. The lowest point of the swing is past the golf ball.

11. Placing the golf ball too far toward the front foot at address. The club reaches the ball in an ascending attitude past the center of the arc, which in this case is too far behind the golf ball. Similar effect as #1b but a different cause.

12. Throwing the clubhead at the ball with the hands in an effort to create greater speed as the clubhead approaches it. This ends up producing the same action as in #1a but for a different cause.

Correction

The first and simplest thing to do if you are prone to top your shots is to brush the grass on which the ball is resting. Realize that if the grass is brushed, since it is below the ball, it is impossible to contact the ball on the top. The club must be returned to the same location it had prior to its being swung, and that location is on the grass behind the ball.

This being a simple quick fix, it may not correct the basic cause of topping, so getting help to determine the real cause is highly recommended so the correction can be permanent.

Once you determine the actual cause of topping, you can apply some rather simple corrections. Check the above 12 points, then check the following corrective procedures that apply to you. You can determine some of these causes yourself, but for others, the eyes of a golf instructor will be necessary. At times, still pictures (for static positions such as the address position and the finish of the swing) can point out some of the faults. For other problems, video-taping might be more helpful.

To correct #1 (a & b) and #3: Your mental picture of the ball flight must be changed. The ball should be visualized flying forward (very low), thus allowing the loft of the club to raise the golf ball. This will eliminate the hand action for the purpose of getting the ball up. Remember that you are trying to send a ball, which is on the ground to a point forward of you that is also on the ground—not in the clouds.

To correct #2: The heel of your back foot must be allowed to rise with the motion of the club. When the club reaches the horizontal level after impact, the back foot should be vertical to the ground.

To correct #4, #5, #6, and #12: Your arms and wrists should be kept tension free so the club is afforded maximum freedom. This freedom is instrumental in producing an efficient and constant motion, with no sudden spurts in an effort to increase speed at the last possible moment.

To correct #7: You should be at such a distance from the ball that when you swing the club, you don't need to reach for the ball. From the end of the backswing, if the club is allowed to fall freely, it should return to the ball so that it is exactly at the center of gravity (the sweet spot) of the clubface.

To correct #8: Your weight should transfer to the front foot as the swing progresses, but only as a response to it. At the moment of impact, the weight should be pretty equal on each foot and will transfer to the front foot as a result of the pull of the centrifugal force created by the swinging motion.

To correct #9: The responsibility for the forward swing should rest with your arms not any other part of your body, though everything must respond in synchronized harmony.

To correct #10 and #11: Place the ball so that when the clubhead is placed next to it at the address position, the clubhead will be at the center of your stance.

Hitting the Ground Behind the Ball

When the clubhead strikes the ground before making contact with the ball, the results can be rather disturbing. The shots have a very bad feel and the distance is far from what is expected. What makes players hit the ground when they are really trying to do something to and with the golf ball? Following are the causes and corrections for this problem.

Trying to get under the ball

Cause

Once a player intends to raise the ball by getting under it, it invades every part of the game. It is not possible to get under the golf ball because the ground is under it, so if you try, you will hit the ground behind the ball. This intent is most prevalent when hitting the lofted irons: 9-iron and the wedges. Because of their loft, these clubs send the ball fairly high, but this height is not your responsibility.

Correction

Change your mental image of the shot to be played. Instead of visualizing the ball going high, visualize it as flying very low, the lower the better.

105

This does not mean that you should make any effort to hit a low shot, it is merely a change in your mental picture—a mental correction.

This mental correction will result in your swing being changed without you making any conscious effort to change it. The physical change will be that you will swing the golf club much more forward instead of moving it downward and then trying to move it upward.

The desire to get the right (left for left-handed players) shoulder under as the swing is started in the forward swing

Cause

This lowers your shoulder so there is no room to swing the club forward, so the ground is struck first.

Correction

You don't need to make any effort to get the shoulder under, that is what it will do automatically if the club is swung forward with the arms in the direction of the target.

The concept of pulling down with the left hand at the beginning of the forward swing

Cause

This pulling action makes the swing too vertical in its approach to the ball, and once the club starts going down, the speed that is generated makes it impossible to change that down direction to a forward direction, so the club will have a tendency to contact the ground behind the golf ball.

Correction

You must return the responsibility for the forward swing to the arms and have them swing the entire golf club forward in the direction of the target.

The desire to add speed as the club approaches the golf ball

Cause

In order to do this, the hands will be used to thrust the head of the club at the ball, the direction of this thrust is downward. Again the ground is struck prior to the clubhead reaching the ball.

Correction

Return the responsibility for the forward swing to the arms and make no effort to change the speed as impact time approaches. Once the forward swing is started, you should not intend to suddenly increase the power at the last minute. The acceleration of the forward swing must be kept very constant.

The use of the upper torso to start the forward swing

Cause

When we try to do this, we lower the upper body, which lowers the center of the swing and does not leave enough room for the club to be swung forward. Thus it strikes the ground behind the ball.

Correction

Return the responsibility for the forward swing to your arms, maintaining the center of the swing (the midpoint between your shoulders) at the same level it was when the address position was taken. Then allow your body to respond, rather than using it to get the club swinging.

Coming Over the Top

Practically everyone who slices his or her shots will eventually develop this problem when swinging the club from the beginning of the forward swing. It is an attempt by the player to keep the ball from slicing. The player's feeling is that if the shoulders are turning in the opposite direction of the ball flight, the ball will not slice. This spinning action of the shoulders is called coming over the top.

Effect

If players could learn that what causes the ball to curve is the spin that the direction of the swing imparts to it, this would not be such a common problem. This spinning action of the shoulders causes the club to approach the ball from the outside of the target line, which imparts to the ball greater side spin, thus causing it to slice even more.

We must differentiate here between the lofted clubs and those with little loft. Loft is very forgiving, so that with clubs such as the 7-, 8-, 9-irons and wedges, this spinning action of the shoulders does not allow the clubhead to give side spin to the ball. Therefore, the shots will be pulled rather than sliced. Once the lofts start decreasing, the potential for side spin increases and with it the degree of slice. Since the driver is the club with least amount of loft, the side spin imparted to the ball is the greatest, so players who come over the top have the most trouble with this club. I constantly hear the comment "I can't hit my driver but I can hit my 4-wood." The extra loft is forgiving. The player makes the same error with both clubs, but the result is very different.

Correction

As great and as common a problem as this is, the correction is quite simple: Swing the club back in a circular pattern so that when it reaches the horizontal level it is parallel to the target line. You must engrave in your mind the direction that is used in your backswing, and as you swing the club forward you must retrace that direction. Retracing the direction of the backswing in the forward swing makes "coming over the top" impossible. You must simply remain aware of that direction while making the swing.

Please do not interpret direction as path. The paths of the backswing and the forward swing are not the same but the direction should be. The path is the road the club takes and the direction is the direction of the road.

The following drill can be used to better understand the corrective procedure. See Figure 16.

Practice Exercise

1. Take the normal address position at the ball.

2. Move the club back about 12 inches keeping the clubhead on the ground. It should describe an arc, not a straight line.

3. Focus on that spot 12 inches from the ball and use it as the starting point for your backswing. Your body should remain facing the original ball position, not the starting point.

4. Swing the club to the end of the backswing.

5. Stop at the end of the backswing.

6. Return the club to the spot 12 inches from the ball.

Figure 16

7. This return movement should be done in slow motion so you can become aware of the direction of the movement back to the spot.

8. Do this drill several times.

9. Now swing the club slowly returning it to that same spot allowing the ball to be sent on its way.

10. Little by little increase the speed, never forgetting the spot to which the club has to be returned.

11. As this change is progressing, and you become aware of the proper direction of the swing, start returning the club closer and closer to the ball until the swing can be started from the ball.

12. Since corrections take time, you will have a tendency to return to the habit of using your shoulders. To continue breaking the bad habit, alternate between starting the swing from the ball and from different spots behind the ball.

13. To solidify the intent to change the direction of the forward swing, even though the swing is started from the ball, you should attempt to return the club to a spot behind the ball.

As the swing direction improves, you will begin to make contact with the spot behind the ball that is being used. This is a good sign. When this happens, the spot behind the ball should be picked closer to the ball, but the direction should remain as corrected. The club will then return to the ball over all the spots selected.

Shanking

Without question, the most disturbing shot a golfer can make is a shank. It bears this name because the place where the shaft is attached to the iron head (the heel of the clubhead) is called the shank, and that is where the golf ball is struck. In the woods, there is no shank, so that a golf ball struck in that area is simply called a heeled shot. The reaction of the two impacts, though both on the heel of the clubhead, could not be more different.

With the woods, the ball will have a tendency to start toward the left of the target and have a tendency to slice with reduced distance. With the irons, however, a heeled or shanked shot shoots sharply to the right at approximately 45° to the intended target line. A most disturbing sight.

Cause

In order to treat a shank as just a missed shot, the cause must be clearly understood. Certainly one does not like to miss a shot in any other category (topping, hooking, slicing), but only the shank causes such fright that players seem to be hypnotized by it and proceed to keep on shanking.

When a ball is struck on the heel of the clubhead, the first thing one has to realize is that the clubhead was returned in the forward swing to a point farther away from the player than where the ball is located. It is just that simple.

Now, once we realize this, we have to determine the reason why the club returns to a point farther away from the player. Here are the causes:

1. Addressing the ball with the weight on the heels.

   When the weight is on the heels, as soon as the player starts to swing, the weight has a tendency to return to the balls of the feet (this is simply good balance). The weight shifts toward the ball. This change in the balance forces the body to move toward the golf ball and the clubhead to go beyond it. When the swing is produced, the player returns the clubhead to a point beyond the golf ball, and the ball will then be struck with the shank.

2. Starting the forward swing with a horizontal rotation of the shoulders.

3. Starting the forward swing with a downward motion of the shoulders, making the clubhead return to a point beyond the ball.

4. Throwing the clubhead toward the ball with the intent of sending it in the opposite direction than that of the previously shanked shot, and at the same time closing the clubface to be sure that the direction of the shot is changed.

5. Being high hand dominant in the backswing making it too flat. At the start of the backswing, the hands and butt end of the club shaft move farther away from the player and the clubhead goes behind the player. In

order to return the clubhead to the ball it has to be moved in a direction which is away from the player and will be closing (see figures 18 & 19).

The first shank the player produces is just an accident—it does not come from a particular defect in the swing and it should not imply there is one. Most players are convinced that the direction of the shanked shot means that the clubface is open at impact. The problem is not the first shank (See Figure 17), it is what the player subsequently attempts to do to keep from shanking again. The player keeps trying to close the clubface, which is a natural reaction to the belief that it was open in order to shank. This is why anyone who shanks has a difficult time correcting the problem. After a player shanks the first shot, the clubface will be closed in all successive shots. See Figure 18 and 19.

Years ago it was easy to prove to someone who shanked that his or her club was closed, because the paint of the ball would register the impact and it would be seen on the inside of the hosel or shank. Had the club been open, the mark would have been left on the outside of the shank of the club, never on the inside

Correction

To correct #1: Simply move away from the ball until your weight feels evenly distributed on your feet.

To correct #2: Return the responsibility for the forward swing to your arms. Your shoulders will then respond naturally and properly to the club's motion.

To correct #3: Return the responsibility for the forward swing to your arms and maintain the center of your swing (the midpoint between your shoulders) at the same level it was at the address position.

A downward motion with your shoulders means that you are bending over more as the swing progresses from the beginning of the forward swing. This additional bending causes the center of the swing to go down and results in your being able to reach beyond the ball.

To correct #4: Return the responsibility for the forward swing to your arms, being aware of returning the clubhead to the ball in the same position and to the same location as it was at the address position. Maintain constant pressure in your hands so they do not get involved in an attempt to close the clubface.

To correct #5: Use both hands equally in the backswing. The low hand is needed to keep the club on its proper plane.

Quick Fix

If no time is available to go to the practice tee to determine the cause of shanking, here is a foolproof quick fix. See Figure 20.

Practice Exercise

Take your normal address position, focus on a spot 1 or 1-1/2 inches from the ball on your side. Keep your eye there and swing at that spot as though it were the ball. Do not allow your intent or your eye to shift to the ball.

Figure 17

Figure 18

Figure 19

Don't be surprised if the first couple of shots that you hit swinging at the spot instead of the golf ball go to the left. This will prove to you that the clubface was being closed to correct the shank.

This procedure should be used if you fear the shot might be shanked. It will work regardless of the cause of your shank and can be used with complete confidence on the golf course.

I have a tendency to shank when hitting a pitch shot around the green when the ball is below my feet. With the ball in this position, my weight seems to be forced forward down the hill toward the golf ball. By using this quick fix method, I never have any problem. By doing this it is impossible to shank.

A Very Important Thing to Remember: *A shanked shot is not produced with an open clubface. If it were open the ball would be struck with the toe of the club, not the heel*

Figure 20

Understand the causes and the corrective procedures of this frightening shot and it will never frighten you again.

Corrections for Incorrect Ball Flight

In the remaining sections of this chapter, the following ball flight patterns are referenced. See diagrams on p. 117.

1. Ball starts straight to the target but then curves to the left.

2. Ball starts straight to the target but then curves to the right.

3. Ball starts to the right of the target and continues straight right.

4. Ball starts to the right of the target and then curves to the right.

5. Ball starts to the right of the target and then curves to the left.

6. Ball starts to the left of the target and continues straight left.

7. Ball starts to the left of the target and then curves to the right.

8. Ball starts to the left of the target and then curves to the left.

Note: *For left-handed players the direction of the ball curve must be reversed.*

1. Ball Starts Straight to the Target but then Curves to the Left.

Analysis

    a.   Club is swinging on target.

    b.   Clubhead is being rolled by the hands at impact.

    c.   Height of shot will be lower than normal.

Correction

Return the responsibility for the forward swing to your arms and have them swing the whole club from the end of the backswing to the end of the swing.

Ball Flight

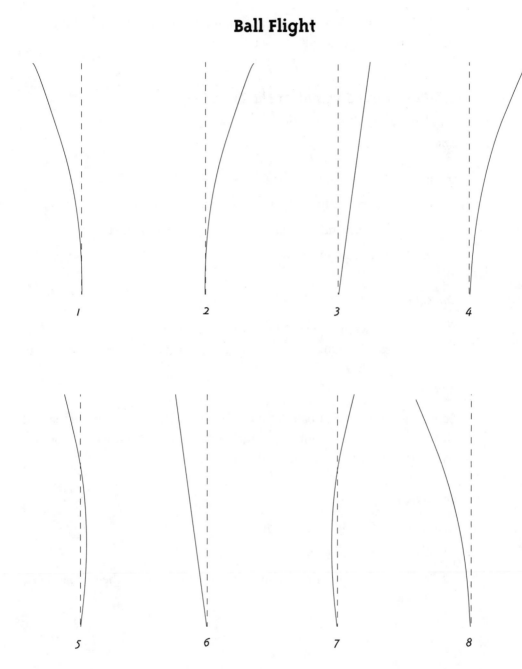

Visualize the toe of the clubhead pointing up and the shaft of the club parallel to the target line halfway to the end of the swing.

2. Ball Starts Straight to the Target but then Curves to the Right

Analysis 1

    a.   Club is swinging on target.

    b.   Clubhead is out of square at impact.

        There is too much rigidity in leading arm and wrist.

    c.   Height of shot is quite normal.

Correction

When club is swung forward, keep your arms and wrists relaxed and flexible. Visualize the club on target with the toe of the clubhead pointing up.

Analysis 2

Sometimes, this type of ball flight can be produced by a premature lateral shift of weight to the front foot, causing the center of the swing to go toward the target too soon. The clubhead will be out of square.

Correction

Maintain your swing center until impact.

1. Become aware of your swing center or
2. Maintain equal weight distribution on your feet until the ball has been struck.

3.   Ball Starts to the Right of the Target and Stays Straight Right

Analysis

   a.   The swinging motion is fine but its direction is to the right.

   b.   Player may have the ball too far toward the back foot with the shoulders facing the ball.

   c.   Player's setup is fine as far as ball and club position is concerned, but the shoulder line points to the right. The swing will be made in the direction of the shoulder line.

Correction

Correct your address position. Then swing the club so that the shaft is parallel to the target line halfway in the backswing and halfway to the end of the swing after impact with the toe of the clubhead pointing up.

4.   Ball Starts to the Right of the Target and then Curves to the Right

Analysis

   a.   Ball flies higher than normal.

   b.   Player is trying to lift the ball.

   c.   Grip is incorrect.

      i. Low hand is too far on top of the shaft.

      ii. High hand is too far under the shaft.

   d.   Player is trying to get the shoulder under the chin in the forward swing.

   e.   Player is using the shoulders to tip the swing and lift the ball.

   f.   Player is using the legs.

g. Player is using the hips in a tilting action.

h. High-hand dominance in the backswing laying the club off, combined with rigidity of the leading arm and wrist in the forward swing.

Correction

Change your mental picture of the shot. Visualize the ball flying forward toward the target, not upward. Correct the grip if necessary. (See Chapter 1 on the Grip.)

If the cause is "d," "e," "f," or "g," return the responsibility for the forward swing to your arms. If the problem is h, you must involve your low hand in the backswing, so both hands are equally involved in swinging the club away from the ball.

5. Ball Starts to the Right of the Target and then Curves to the Left

Analysis

a. Club is swung inside out with the hands producing a rolling action at impact.

b. The player may be trying to get the shoulder under the chin in the forward swing and in so doing changes the shoulder line to the right. This is coupled with a rolling action of the clubhead as in "a."

c. Trying to keep the elbow of the trailing arm close to the body in the forward swing, which turns out to be the same as "b."

Correction

Give your arms the responsibility for the forward swing and remember to have the club shaft parallel to the target line with the toe of the clubhead pointing up halfway in the backswing and halfway to the end of the swing after impact.

6. *Ball Starts to the Left of the Target and Stays Straight Left*
Analysis

    a.   The swinging motion is fine but the direction is to the left.

    b.   Player may have the ball too far toward the front foot with the shoulders facing the ball.

Correction

Correct your address position so that the clubhead is in the center between your feet and your body is facing the clubface squarely. Swing the club in the direction of the target with your arms. When the club reaches a horizontal level halfway in the backswing and halfway to the end of the swing after impact, it should be parallel to the target line with the toe of the clubhead pointing up.

7. *Ball Starts to the Left of the Target and then Curves to the Right*
Analysis

    a.   Ball may be placed too far toward the back foot with the shoulder line on the same plane as the target line, causing the club to be out of square, facing to the right (left for left-handed players.)

    b.   Club is swung outside the target line both backward and forward.

    c.   Backswing is correct but the shoulders are used in a horizontal manner to start the forward swing.

    d.   Backswing is correct but the hips are used in a spinning action to start the forward swing.

Correction

Correct your address position by placing the clubhead in the center of the stance and the body facing the clubface squarely.

For "b," "c," and "d," your arms must assume the responsibility for the forward swing so that the shaft of the club is parallel to the target line halfway in the backswing and halfway to the end of the swing after impact, with the toe of the clubhead pointing up.

8. Ball Starts to the Left of the Target and then Curves to the Left

Analysis

    a.   The club is swung outside the target line with the hands rolling the clubhead closed at impact.

    b.   The backswing is correct but at the beginning of the forward swing, the shoulders are used, thus changing the direction of the swing to the left, then adding a rolling action of the clubhead with the hands at impact.

Note: *If the ball is placed too far to the front foot, the reaction will be much greater.*

Correction

Correct your address position if necessary.

For "a" and "b" your arms must assume responsibility for the forward swing so that the shaft is parallel to the target line halfway in the backswing and halfway to the end of the swing, with the toe of the clubhead pointing up.

It must appear to you that the same type of corrections are being used over and over again.

Here are the reasons why.

• The use of your arms prevents any rolling action of your hands, which give the clubhead the rolling action. Using your arms will prevent hand use.

- The concept of the shaft parallel to the target line at the halfway points of the backswing and the end of the swing after impact adjusts the direction of the swing and puts it on target.

- Finally, with the toe of the clubhead pointing up, square impact is possible.

By putting these three facts together, all shots should be greatly improved and a high degree of consistency can be achieved.

When working on having the club parallel to the target line halfway in the backswing and halfway to the end of the forward swing after impact, remember that the clubface must return to the ball at 90 degrees (square) to the target line. Simply visualizing the clubhead toe up to toe up is not sufficient. It must be visualized toe up, square, and toe up.

Part IV

Special Shots

Chapter 6

Sand Play

The game of golf has two types of sand shots. One is called the *explosion shot*, which is played when the golf ball is in a bunker located around the green (a greenside bunker). It is called an explosion shot because the clubhead strikes the sand instead of the ball, forcing the sand where the ball is resting out of the bunker. The second type is a shot from a bunker from which distance is necessary. In this shot you must not strike the sand before the ball—clean contact between clubface and golf ball is necessary.

For this part of the discussion, let us assume that the ball in the bunker is resting on top of the sand on a very level lie.

According to the rules of golf, when taking your stance in a sand bunker, grounding the club on the sand is not allowed. The clubhead must be kept above the sand during address, and the clubhead must not touch the sand at any time in the backswing. Should you inadvertently touch the sand at address or in the backswing, a two-stroke penalty will be incurred. So be careful.

Keep the club above the sand at address by bending your arms, not by standing more erect. By bending your arms, when the club is swung forward, the centrifugal force created will straighten the arms allowing the clubhead to reach the sand. If you keep the club above the sand by standing more erect, your arms are already extended so the clubhead will not be able to reach the sand, causing shots without any sand cushion between the clubface and the ball. This will make the ball go very far and makes it impossible to make the nice high soft shot which is needed from greenside bunkers.

I also recommend that you use your feet to pack the sand under them, so that when you make your swing, the sand does not give way causing you to lose your balance. This work of the feet is not intended to bury your feet in the sand in order to keep them motionless. The heel of your back foot should rise as a response to the forward swing in exactly the same way it does in a regular shot from grass. At the end of the swing the sole of your back foot should be vertical to the ground whether it be grass or sand, and you should finish erect, facing the target.

Figure 21

The Address Position for Greenside Bunker Shots

Normal address position is the same as for any other club. See Figure 21.

a. Club in the center of the stance.

b. Weight evenly distributed on the feet.

c. Ball is placed slightly forward of normal. This makes it easier to pick up an adequate amount of sand.

d. If you wish to play the bunker shot with the clubface open, the alignment should be moved to the left.

When an address position is taken with the clubface open, you must consider two directions. First is the direction of the swing and second is the direction projected from the clubface.

The body is aligned to the left, because of this, the swing is directed to the left of the target. The clubface will be facing to the right, causing the ball to go to the right. When the club is in motion, these two directions compromise and the ball is directed forward in a direction in between the two and this will end up being the direction to the target.

The Address Position for Fairway Bunker Shots

Normal address position is the same as for any other club.

a. Start with club in the center of the stance.

b. Weight evenly distributed on the feet.

c. Ball is placed slightly back of normal. The proper way to place the club behind the ball is to simply move the clubhead behind the ball without moving anything else. The body should be facing the spot where the ball would be if the ball were placed normally.

d. If the height of the shot is not an issue, that is, if the bank of the bunker you have to carry is not very high, place the clubface at right angle to the target line. This will produce a fairly low shot.

e. If the height of the shot is an issue, that is, if you are facing a high bank, then place the clubface behind the golf ball in a fanned position. With this clubface position you must be aligned more to the left.

Greenside Bunker Shots

Getting the Right Mental Attitude

When players go into a greenside bunker to play a sand shot and I ask them—What is on your mind, what do you want to do? The answer without exception is: "I want to get out." This is the most detrimental thought players can have. The proper intent is to go into that bunker to play a sand shot. Why should the idea of getting out be so detrimental for successful sand play and what should the proper mental attitude be?

First, in a greenside bunker, the golf club does not get the ball out because it never makes contact with it. There is always a cushion of sand between the clubface and the ball—the ball really rides on the sand and the sand lifts the ball out of the bunker.

When we try to "get out," our mind translates that attitude into a scooping action, resulting in the clubhead getting ahead of the grip end of the shaft and the loft of the club greatly increased. See Figure 22a.

Even though we may be in a bunker with a high bank to go over, our intent should still be to send the ball forward to the target. To be successful in sand play, visualize the scraped sand sending the ball forward and burying it in the bank of the bunker. See Figure 22b. This image should counteract any intent to *get out.*" Trying to scoop the ball out has the following results:

1. You catch the ball without any sand and send it over the green.

2. If you do take sand, the ball goes a very short distance or remains in the bunker because the added loft given to the clubface makes it slide under the ball so there is no forward motion imparted to the golf ball. The speed necessary to produce a successful shot is decreased.

The reasons for these results are as follows:

1. The first result above can be explained using straight lines. Suppose you had a piece of wood measuring 4 feet in length, with a hinge at the midpoint. If you bend that piece

Figure 22a

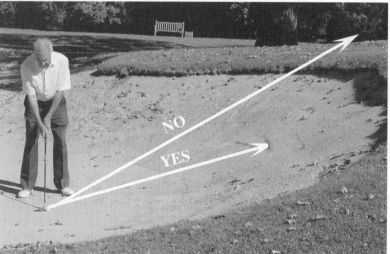

Figure 22b

of wood, the ends are no longer 4 feet apart. The distance between the two ends has been decreased. The closer to 90° the two halves are, the closer the ends of the piece of wood are.

In the golf swing, if you consider a straight line to the golf ball from the midpoint between the shoulders, that is the equivalent to the piece of wood. The hinge in the piece of wood is equivalent to the human hinge, the wrists.

Now consider a second straight line. The line starts at the midpoint between the shoulders, but now this line goes to the clubhead. If the ball and the clubhead are to meet, these two lines must measure exactly the same length. If a scooping action is used, an angle is created at the hinge and that angle shortens the length of the line from the midpoint between the shoulders to the clubhead. However, the length of the line between the midpoint of the shoulders to the golf ball has remained the same. This change in length of the line from the midpoint between the shoulders and the clubhead makes the player catch the ball clean (with no sand). If you did this on the fairway instead of the bunker, the shot would also be topped.

2. The second result—loss of speed—is easy to understand. If two objects are moving in the same direction, in order for one to pass the other, the object doing the passing has to be going faster than the other one.

In the golf swing the arms slow down when the scooping action takes place and the clubhead passes the arms and hands. If your arms slow down, there is no way you can generate the desired speed.

To be a good bunker player, the swing produced with the sand iron should be exactly the same as that used to play any other shot. The only difference is the size of the swing. No other changes are necessary. Because of the resistance of the sand as the clubhead goes through it, the size of the swing to send the ball a particular distance is much larger than it would be if the ball were sent the same distance from the grass. There is no direct contact between the clubface and the golf ball when playing an explosion shot.

During the execution there is the intent of scraping the sand, where in the regular shot off the grass, the intent is to brush the grass. Don't be concerned with where the sand has to be contacted, each person's scraping feel is good enough. Some instructors advise their students to contact the sand 1 or 2 inches behind the ball, but when they execute the actual sand shot, they contact the sand much earlier than that.

When I have taught the sand shot to both professionals and amateurs, established players or advanced beginners, I have them make three swings and ask them to contact the sand 2 inches behind the ball. Unfortunately they are unable to do it—they contact the sand at different distances from the ball. If these contact points are joined by a line going from contact point to contact point, it turns out to be a very jagged line.

However, if I ask the same players to simply scrape the sand without any concern as to where they are going to scrape it, the points of contact with the sand are at the same distance from the ball, so that if these points are joined they form a very straight line. This shows great consistency.

The concept of scraping the sand, rather than hitting the sand, not only makes it very easy to play out of greenside bunkers regardless of the sand condition, be it deep or shallow, but it forces the motion to be made in a forward direction.

Fairway Bunker Shots

Distance is necessary in fairway bunker shots. They can be played as full shots, half, or three-quarter shots depending on the distance needed and can be played with any club. Sand must not be caught between the ball and clubface.

For players with great experience and club control as well as self-control, they can simply pick the ball clean without making any changes. Their mental discipline enables them to perform this without difficulty. Most players, however, are not included in this relatively small group, and they need some help to perform this shot well.

You can do one of three things to make a good fairway bunker shot—all produce the same results.

1. Make your swing more forward than normal, as though the ball were approximately 2 inches forward of where it is located.

2. Place the ball slightly back of center at the address position with the balance of the address position unchanged. The easiest way to do this is to take the normal stance with the clubhead addressing a spot on the sand about two inches to the target side of the ball. With the ball placed this way, swing at the spot that was addressed originally. See Figure 23. By swinging at the spot in front of the ball, you make clean contact with it and obtain distance.

3. Take your normal address position but instead of keeping the clubhead above the sand by bending your arms, raise your shoulders so that your arms are fully extended. This is called using a higher center to play this shot. With your arms so extended, the clubhead cannot get into the sand and meets the ball without any sand between the clubface and the ball. You have to experiment with the amount you have to raise your shoulders, because if you raise them more than necessary, the ball can be topped. If your shoulders are not raised enough, the clubhead will catch the sand. The shoulders should be raised so that when your arms are extended, the bottom of the clubface is above the sand but slightly below the center (equator) of the ball. When the swing is made, the center must remain at the high level it was set at the address position. Use the normal swing—do not change anything.

Figure 23

132

Chipping From Greenside Bunkers

If the ball is very well placed in the bunker and the bank in front of you is very low, it is possible to play a chip shot from the sand. Another situation that makes chipping from bunkers a possibility is if the ball is on a sidehill where the target foot is higher than the back foot. With this type of side-hill lie, the sand is well below the ball on the contact side, so a chip shot could be preferable.

You can modify your address position in the same way as in #3 above for chipping out of fairway bunkers. Chip shots from bunkers can be played successfully with a high center.

The direction of the swinging motion has to be forward. If there is any tendency to swing downward, the club will strike the sand first and this will destroy the chip. The ball must be contacted before the sand.

Exploded Chip Shots From Greenside Bunkers

Certain situations may require special adaptations in order to execute a successful shot. If the greenside bunker is very shallow and the flagstick is very close to the edge of the green as well as to you, so that you don't have much room on the green to work with, the best shot to play is an exploded chip shot. The address position for this type of shot is the same as for a regular explosion shot, and you simply play a chip shot the same way as if the ball were on grass, but scraping the sand with the same intent as in the regular explosion shot. The resulting shot will be very short and very delicate. From an apparent difficult shot due to the lack of green to work with, the exploded chip shot turns it into a very easy shot to perform.

Exploded chip shots are also excellent shots to use when the ball is in a shallow bunker and the green is tilted away from you. With these conditions the ball has to fall on the green very softly and with very little forward motion. The exploded chip shot will accomplish this.

Important Points for Explosion Shots

The swings from greenside bunkers are much larger than they would be if the ball were sent the same distance from grass. The swing should be completed, finished as though a driver swing was being made. If the swing is abbreviated (cut off), the swing speed is diminished and that, coupled with the resistance of the sand, makes the ball carry a shorter distance than needed. If an explosion shot has to go a very short distance, players have a greater tendency to make this abbreviated swing.

It is very helpful to visualize the clubface as it travels through the sand, and this depends on the shot being played. The face of the club can be set in a position that is square with the target line, in which case as it travels through the sand, it will remain square, and then proceed to a toe up position past the ball.

Some of us like to play these explosion shots with an open blade because a higher and softer bunker shot with less roll can be produced that way. When most people try to learn this type of bunker shot, not only do they set the clubhead open, but they open it further as they swing and the clubhead just slides through the sand under the ball and they remain in the bunker. Even though the clubhead may be placed open, the club should be swung with the intent of having the clubhead be toe up toward the target on the way to a full finish. Of course, it will not be 100% toe up. At the moment the club points forward at the horizontal level, the clubhead will be open to the same degree it was open when it was gripped.

Should the Sand Wedge always be Used in Greenside Bunkers?

No, it is sometimes advisable to use other clubs in order to obtain better results. The conditions at hand should dictate what club to use. Study the conditions for the shot, and evaluate the possible options and which one of those possible options best fits the shot to be made.

For example, if a ball is in a bunker and there is a tree in front of you, and the branches overhang so that they are between the ball and the flagstick, it would be foolish to use the sand wedge. This club would send the ball into the branches and could end up in a worse position than it was in the bunker. A better club for these conditions would be a 7-iron, which would send the ball low and give it a little run so that it would miss the branches and get to the hole.

Another example is a long explosion shot. Long explosion shots are difficult to judge because most of the time the player feels that less sand has to be taken in order to get the distance. In trying to do this most of the time, no sand is taken and the ball is flown over the green. Here again 5-, 6-, 7-, 8- or 9-irons can be used depending on your confidence level as well as the distance the explosion shot has to travel. Use these clubs exactly the same way as the sand iron—scraping the sand is a must.

If a ball is resting on the front bank of a greenside bunker, even though it may be slightly embedded, a 7-iron is a better club to use than a sand wedge. To play this shot, the ball is placed toward your back foot and your weight is kept on the front foot. Swing the club with an exaggerated backward and forward motion so that the clubhead enters the sand on a very horizontal level. Swing the club into the bank—there will be no follow-through. Any downward tendency in the swing will destroy this shot. 5- and 6-irons can also be used for this shot.

Bad Lies In Bunkers

When the ball in the bunker is buried (not on the banks) in a fried egg lie or in a footprint, or if a mound of sand is behind the ball, you must make an adjustment in your swing. The clubhead has to be driven below the golf ball to allow the sand to send the ball out of the bunker. To accomplish this, the swing has to be made more vertical, both in the backswing and the forward swing. The ball should be placed toward the back foot and the clubhead should be delofted so that it is at a right angle to the target line. See Figure 24.

By delofting the clubface, the bounce of the sole is eliminated and the sand iron will now have a cutting edge (the bottom line of the clubface), which is needed to penetrate the sand to get beneath the ball. Delofting the clubface is not closing it. If in attempting to deloft the clubface, you should close it, the shot will come out to the left of the target.

The swing must be quite strong because the clubhead has to be driven deep into the sand. If the ball is deep in the sand, you should not attempt to finish the swing normally. Because the movement is so vertical, the club should be left in the sand.

Figure 24

Very Deep Greenside Bunkers

Whenever the ball falls in a very deep greenside bunker, the first thing that comes to the player's mind is "I have to hit it very high." The player sees the very high bank on the way to the hole and there is a tremendous desire to get the ball over it.

When facing this type of shot, you need to realize that the shot needed is not a higher shot but a longer one, and your success rate will be much higher. Remember that the law of trajectory says that the longer the object is propelled, the higher it goes. Acting with this knowledge in mind, the ball will automatically go higher without any intent of sending it higher. Therefore, if you find yourself in a very deep greenside bunker, make a bigger swing so you execute a longer bunker shot. You will be pleasantly surprised— the ball will not go too far because you are sending the ball to an elevated green.

Remember that you must use the sand to play the shot; you do not want to catch the ball clean, without any sand.

Greenside Bunker Lies on Hard Surface

Sometimes the ball lands in a greenside bunker on a hard surface with very little sand or on packed sand. If a player tends to want to lift the ball out of a bunker, these two types of lies will increase that desire. Your attitude should not change because of the lie, but some adjustments can be made to facilitate a successful shot. If the sand is hard, the sand iron will have a tendency to bounce on the hard surface, catch the ball in the middle, and line it over the green.

You should use the same setup as if the ball were buried in the sand. Place the ball off center toward your back foot, deloft the club, and use a more vertical swing. The swing will now be more up and down rather than back and forth. The delofting of the sand iron takes the bounce out of the sole and gives it more of a cutting edge so that when the more up and down movement is made, the cutting edge can dig deeper into the sand and reach a point below the golf ball. This requires a very strong action.

Because the swing is so vertical, there should be no attempt to finish the swing in the normal way. The club should be left buried in the sand.

With packed sand the situation is not so demanding because, even though it is packed from rain or from watering the green, there is still an adequate amount of sand. The moment the club touches the sand, it breaks up and it will act as loose sand. However, bear in mind that wet sand is heavier, so make your swing bigger so the size will produce the greater speed needed to travel through the heavy wet sand.

For these types of lies, sometimes using a pitching wedge produces good results because there is no bounce construction on pitching wedges. Without having to adjust the address or the clubface positions, the cutting edge already exists in these clubs.

Sidehill Lies in Bunkers

The Front Foot Higher Than the Back Foot

If your lie in the bunker is such that your front foot is higher than your back foot, the sand behind the ball is lower than the ball, so the clubhead must be placed lower than the ball but not on the sand. See Figure 25. The adjustment is necessary if an exploded chip shot is to be played. If the ball were addressed as if it were on a level surface, it would be caught clean and sent a long way. If a chip shot is to be played from that position, the adjustment is not necessary, so the ball can be caught first without any sand. See Figure 26.

Figure 25   *Figure 26*

The Back Foot Higher Than the Front Foot

When the back foot is higher than the front foot, whether in sand or grass, the ball is always placed off center toward the high foot, which means the shot will be considerably lower.

I consider this to be the most difficult shot in the game of golf. If the bank in front of the player has any degree of height, with this type of address position it is not possible to attain the necessary elevation in the shot to clear the bank. If by chance you clear the bank, the ball comes out driving and rolls over the green. This type of shot demands a tremendous amount of practice just to be able to keep the ball on the green.

For most players, I recommend that, instead of making the shot in the direction of the high bank to go to the flagstick, the shot be directed either backward (away from the green) or to the side. The important thing to do is to get the ball to leave the sand. Applying this method, you can get the ball out in one stroke.

From a lie where your back foot is the high foot, by turning around and going backward, the back foot now becomes the low foot, and you have turned the most difficult shot in the game into the easiest shot in the game. The ball can now be rolled out of the sand even with your putter.

If it bothers you to have to go over the bunker in the next shot, you can play the bunker shot far enough to the side so that the bunker is no longer an issue. Remember that saving strokes is the name of the game— the more strokes you can save, the lower your score. If by using this method strokes can be saved, making a par or bogey possible, it certainly pays to go backward or sideways.

My Personal Opinion

I feel that the more we use the same swing, the more successful we can be. Imagine if you used the method to play sand shots where the club is taken back on the outside and rerouted to the inside, or left on the outside in order to use an outside in pattern. You may have read that some instructors advocate this method, and some of the tour players also use it. But think of this.

Suppose you subscribe to the outside in method. Then you practice it for several days in order to execute it successfully. After you finish practicing the bunker shot, try and play your driver. Can you see that the driver cannot be swung in this manner unless, of course you wish to become a slicer. You will have two completely different swings.

With the method I advocate, which is never change your swing, you could practice your bunker shots and only bunker shots, or any other shots for that matter, for thirty days without practicing your driver. Then if you decide to practice with your driver, you will have been practicing the swing you must use with it during the same thirty days.

Remember that every golfer wants his or her game to be consistent. Consistency means doing the same thing every time—all shots can be played with the same swing and the same set of principles.

I have never felt the need, in my entire golf career, to change my swing to play sand shots. I have never felt the need to change my swing to play any other types of shots. To me it makes sense to have and perfect one swing rather than to have two or three swings.

Chapter 7

Pitching and Chipping

When is a shot a pitch and when is it a chip? A pitch shot stays in the air longer than it is on the ground. A chip stays on the ground longer than it stays in the air. Chipping is what you do near the green, from approximately 10 yards to a few inches. Pitching is what you do when the distance from the ball to the edge of the green is greater than the distance from the edge of the green to the flagstick. A chip has a very short carry and a pitch has a much longer carry.

Regardless of how well you execute the full, three-quarter, and half shots, pitching and chipping are a most important part of the game. Unfortunately, the average player practices the short game less than any other part of the game, yet, a player cannot score without it. It seems that golfers enjoy a long drive or a long iron shot much more than making a small shot well, so that it ends close enough to the hole for one putt.

Through practice, you must develop the ability to take no more than two strokes to complete a hole after having missed a green. This is known as getting up and down. The short game should be much easier than the long game with respect to execution, because it is produced through such a small arc. The speed developed is much less than in a full shot, so it should be much easier to observe and follow the motion. In spite of this expected ease, why do most average players have such great difficulty with it? The reasons are several.

If a drive goes 10 yards to the right or left of the target, we don't seem to take much notice. If we do observe it, not much of an issue is made of those 10 yards.

But if we pitch or chip, and the ball ends up 20 feet from the hole, it is almost a calamity—we are greatly disappointed. Therefore, when playing the short game, more pressure is placed on the ability to execute the shot correctly. This pressure is less on the long shots because we realize it is not very realistic to expect the ball to end up 2 feet from the hole from 200 yards away (although the desire to have it happen is still there). But with the short game, if the ball is 30 feet from the green, we not only desire to have the ball go into the hole, we expect it. But with little or no practice.

Although the stroke is simple and easy to produce, the results obtained depend on each player's feel and judgment. The only way to develop feel and judgment is through practice, lots of practice. Knowledge of the conditions of the surface upon which the ball is to land greatly influences the result, so the knack of determining these conditions must be developed. Again, the requirement for obtaining this knowledge is practice, and through this practice experience in judging properly.

The most common cause for difficulties in the short game is that the mental image of the shot is too high. The height of the shot is produced by the loft, which the manufacturer gave the pitching clubs. It is not produced by the player. See Figure 27.

When we visualize the shot higher than it should be, it causes us to use a scooping action, thereby increasing the loft of the club to produce a high shot. This scooping action is produced with the hands and can make the club meet the ball with the sole line and high on the ball, causing a lined shot, which sends the ball over the green. The scooping action can also produce a very short shot if the player happens to slide the clubface underneath the ball, in which case the club does not impart a forward direction to the ball.

Another way to try to get the ball to fly high is to swing the club in an upward direction, toward the sky. The result is a topped shot.

When a chip shot or pitch shot is hit along the ground, a frequent comment is "I did not get under it." When the shot is attempted again with the intent of getting under the ball, the club strikes the ground behind the ball before contacting the ball. The ground is under the ball, so the player cannot get the club under the ball, it will hit the ground first. This shot is known as a fat shot.

Figure 27

Just as with the long game, pitches and chips must propel the ball forward toward the target, even though lofted clubs are used. The target is never to be found up in the clouds.

Regardless of the distance of the short shots, we must understand the laws of trajectory. This understanding will be of great help in developing a sound short game. The laws are as follows: *In propelling an object, the longer the distance it is sent, the higher it will go. The shorter the distance it is sent, the lower it will go.*

143

Practice Exercise

Take three balls in your hand and throw them to someone one at a time. Throw the first one when the person is 2 feet away and then have that person move farther away and throw the second one, then throw the last one after that person has moved a fairly good distance away. Notice what happens to the height of the throw. Without consciously trying to do anything but throw the ball to that person, as the distance from you gets greater, the longer the distance the ball was thrown, the higher it went.

Shorter shots should be visualized flying lower than long shots.

You should always visualize the ball flying low to the target, even though the club being used, the wedge for example, will send the ball with plenty of height. The lower the shot is visualized, the better the shot will be. See Figure 27. Permit the loft of the club to do the job it was built to do.

Stance for the Short Game

For normal shots, the ball is located so that when it is addressed, the clubhead will be in the center of your stance—just the same as for any other standard or normal shot. See Figure 28. The center of your stance is that point where a perpendicular line from the midpoint between your shoulders touches the ground.

Quite a few players prefer to play these shots with an open stance. In an open stance, the front foot is farther from the target line than the back foot. If you use an open stance, your shoulders must be set so that they are on the same plane as the target line. If your shoulders were level, then your shoulder line and the target line would be parallel.

The Swing for the Chip Shots and Pitch Shots

As I have repeated over and over again, the swing is made with the same purpose as any other swing, for any other shot. The swinging concept

Figure 28

does not change. The swings for short shots are simply smaller than those needed for long shots. The club is swung backward and forward in the direction of the target. When the club reaches the horizontal level in the backswing and the forward swing, the shaft should be parallel to the target line and the toe of the clubhead should be pointing to the sky . . . no different than in any other swing.

When the short shots are played, players tend to stay flatfooted, to not allow the heel of the back foot to rise with the motion. Although players feel that this is too much motion, it is not—the heel is merely responding to the motion of the club. This response is necessary to be able to finish the swing with the body erect and facing the target.

Procedure for Playing a Short Shot

1. Visualize the ball being sent forward toward the target with a low trajectory no matter which club is being used to make the shot.

2. Make the proper club selection.

3. Whenever possible, the ball should land on the green.

4. Determine whether the needed shot is a chip shot or a pitch shot.

5. Evaluate influence of flagstick placement on the decision.

6. Determine the condition of the landing surface. Apply the following rule of thumb although it may be altered by conditions. When the distance between the ball and the edge of the green is equal to or greater than the distance between the edge of the green and the hole, use the lofted clubs—8- or 9-iron or wedges. The greater the distance from the ball to the edge of the green in relation to the distance between the edge of the green and the hole, the more loft should be used. The more lofted clubs produce a higher and softer shot, which will have less roll.

When the distance between the ball and the edge of the green is less than the distance from the edge of the green to the hole, the less lofted clubs should be used—2-, 3-, 4-, 5-, 6- or 7-irons. The shorter the distance from the ball to the edge of the green in relation to the distance from the edge of the green to the hole, the less loft should be used. The less lofted clubs impart more roll to the ball. The rolling shots should be played more often than they are. It is easier to roll the ball to a certain spot than to send it high to a point and expect the ball to stop dead on it.

Practice Exercise

To prove this point, take a ball and throw it underhand so that it stops next to a selected target on the ground. Notice that you will roll it to the selected point most of the way. You will not throw it way up in the air to land and stop next to your target. This normal attitude should be retained when playing the short game.

Examples of Conditions for Club Selection

This example and its variations show conditions and particular situations that determine the majority of club selections.

1. Ball is 30 feet from the green.
2. Hole is 60 feet from the front edge of the green.
3. No hazards to go over to reach the green.
4. Green has normal texture and firmness—no grain.
5. Level green.
6. Ball is well situated on the grass—good lie.

Under these conditions, the suggested club is the 7-iron. Let us now change some of the situations in above example.

1. Increase #1 to 60 feet—suggested new club selection: wedge
2. Decrease #1 to 10 feet—suggested new club selection: 5-iron
3. Decrease #1 to 5 feet—suggested new club selection: 3-iron
4. Increase #2 to 80 feet—suggested new club selection: 5-iron
5. Change #2 to 10 feet—suggested new club selection: wedge
6. Change #2 to 40 feet—suggested new club selection: 9-iron
7. Change #3 to hazard between ball and green—new club selection: wedge
8. Change #4 to very firm green—new club selection: wedge

9. Change #5 to very fast green, downhill from player—new club selection: wedge

10. Change #5 to very fast green, uphill from player—new club selection: 9-iron

11. Change #5 to slow green, downhill from player—new club selection: 8-iron

12. Change #5 to slow green, uphill from player—new club selection: 6-iron

13. Change #6 to ball is in bad lie—new club selection: 6-iron

14. Change #5 to green elevated 10 feet—new club selection: wedge

I'm not implying that these club selections are a must. Different players will have different interpretations of above changes in relation to their ability, preference of shots, and club selections. Some players can play the same club and are able to handle some of the changes listed without changing clubs. However, for players who are not as proficient, it is easier to select clubs that, within themselves, adjust to the new situations. Except when there is a hazard between you and the green, you have quite a number of options depending on your ability, feel, preference, and satisfaction. The example above merely shows how changes in conditions and situations can alter club selection.

Club selection is controlled by shot selection, which in turn is controlled by the situations and conditions of the moment.

Club Selection

Club selection depends upon:

1. Type of shot that can be played

2. Type of shot you wish to play

3. Conditions:

    a.   Hard or soft greens

    b.   Is green elevated or not

    c.   Lie of the ball

    d.   What is between the ball and the green

    e.   Flagstick placement

Conditions control #1. If the ball is located so that the branches from a tree overhang the line of flight the ball will take, high shots cannot be played. Only low shots will be successful in getting past the branches. If conditions allow for several types of shots, then you select the one that will produce the best results.

If the flagstick is located close to the front edge of the green, the best option is to play a low running shot and use the grass on the fairway to slow the ball down and have it trickle slowly to the hole. Playing a high shot to land on the green would not result in a shot that would be able to stop near the hole—there is too short a distance between the edge of the green and the hole to be able to handle that type of shot.

If the flagstick is located at the back of the green, you have a great number of options. Almost any iron will produce shots that can end close to the hole. Under these conditions pitch shots or pitch and run shots can be used and be equally successful. In many cases the pitch and run will produce better results than high pitch shots.

Whenever the ball is in a bad lie, it is best not to try to play high pitch shots. It is much better to use clubs with less loft and play pitch and run shots. There is a great tendency from bad lies to try to lift the ball, resulting in shots that are lined and sent over the green. Sometimes a high shot is required even though the ball is in a bad lie—a bunker or water may be between the ball and the green. When this hazard exists, remember to visualize the shot flying low and allow the loft of the club to send the ball over the bunker or over the water. Any effort from the player to force the ball over those hazards will certainly make the ball fall into them.

The Landing Spot

Is the landing spot of a chip shot or a pitch shot important? Yes, very important, because it controls the type of shot you will play and therefore, your club selection. Once these two decisions have been made, the landing spot should be ignored and only the overall distance to the hole should be kept in mind.

If you concentrate on the landing spot while executing the shot, you will tend to leave the ball short of the hole or to send it too far. By including the landing spot in the shot selection, and the club fitted to that selection, the only thing the player must do is visualize the ball stopping at the hole. The ball will then land in the vicinity of the selected landing spot and although it may not be exact, the ball will be sent the desired distance.

To be accurate in the short game, just as in the long game, you must have a very clear picture of where the target is located. On a very level green, the mind should see the exact location of the hole. On a rolling green, the mind should see a spot even with the hole that takes into consideration the amount of break of the shot. With breaking chips, the eye should not go to the hole prior to making the stroke. If it does, the shot will be either pushed or pulled depending on which way the ball should roll. When playing a break, the hole is no longer the target—the target is that spot to which you are directing the shot.

Warning:: *Do not get involved in determining the size of your swing or how hard to hit the shot. Through practice your mind will learn to interpret what your eyes see and will fit the swing size and the swing speed to the distance the chip shot or pitch shot is to go. However, you will not succeed if you ignore the location of the target while making the stroke.*

Changing Ball Flight

Changes in ball flight are the player's option. If you want to play a higher than normal shot, the ball is placed slightly toward the front foot. See Figure 29. At the address position, place the clubhead as though the ball

Figure 29   *Figure 30*

were in the normal position, which means that the clubhead will be in the center of your stance but slightly behind the ball, not next to the ball. Make your swing as though the ball were next to the clubhead, directing the swing to the spot originally addressed, not to the ball. This type of setup will increase the height of the shot.

If you want to play a lower than normal shot, then the ball is placed slightly toward the back foot. See Figure 30. To take your stance, place the clubhead slightly in front of the ball and take a normal stance with the club-head in the center of the stance. Then just place the clubhead behind the ball without moving anything else, and keep the clubface at a right angle to

151

the target line. This will result in having the butt end of the shaft slightly ahead of the ball. Your body will be facing the spot in front of the ball where the clubhead was placed first, and that is where the swing is directed, not to the ball. This type of setup will decrease the height of the shot.

Do not place the ball toward the back foot and attempt to play a high soft shot. This conflicts with the setup. Whenever the ball is moved toward the back foot, the shot will lose height. This is true with any club.

Ball Resting Against or Close to the High Cut

When the ball is resting against or close to the high cut or fringe around the green, you can use several clubs. However, some clubs can be used with greater success than others. Fairway woods can be used, but because of their length they seem rather unwieldy to some players. The sand iron can also be used, but the ball must be contacted at its equator by the bottom edge of the sand iron. This requires a fine touch.

The easiest club to use is the putter, but a special setup and action are necessary. The ball must be placed toward the back foot and, depending on the height of the grass behind the ball, it may have to be placed outside of the stance. The putter should be placed behind the ball facing the ground (very closed). Because of the ball being so far toward the back foot, the movement of the club will be very much up and down. The movement should be made as though the putter is to hit the ball into the ground. It should be a very gentle tap because the ball will roll with a great deal of overspin because of the pinching action of the ball against the ground, which will make it roll quite a distance. This is easy to do, it works very well, and can be used for both short and long distances.

Ball In Hole Near Green but Not In Its Own Pitch Mark

If the ball is in a hole near the green, but not in its own pitch mark, the only club that will give good results is the putter. The setup is the same as the case where the ball is on the fringe next to the high cut. The ball is placed toward the back foot outside of the stance, the putter closed facing the ground. The movement of the club is up and down as though the ball is to be driven further into the hole. The ball will pop out of the hole beautifully. It will come out of the hole with a great deal of overspin and will be able to roll a long way. The stroke should be made quite gently.

Do not use pitching wedges or sand irons for this shot.

The Gravity Shot

If the ball is off the green but deep in the high cut, it presents some serious concerns for most players. The shot appears much more difficult than it really is, but it requires something a bit different.

When a ball is deep in the grass, it tends to come out with overspin, so it rolls quite a bit once it lands on the green. The overspin and roll happen because there is a great deal of grass between the face of the club and the ball. But the shot you need has to come out very softly and with very little run—so how to accomplish that? From such a position I have tried a great number of different types of shots, and only one comes out as required. Play the shot with a sand iron. The weight of the flange is most helpful in this situation. You make your backswing as with any other shot, but your forward swing is quite different. Once the backswing has been completed, the club must be allowed to fall so that the clubhead buries itself in the grass where the ball lies and stops there. There is no follow-through. You must not be involved in stopping the club nor in forcing it down, any such involvement will destroy the shot. This is why I call it a gravity shot. The club simply falls into the grass and stays in the grass. When the club falls it does not fall vertically, it falls in a forward direction or it will not get to the ball.

This type of action allows the clubhead to get below the ball and lift it out high and with a very soft landing. Absolutely no force is needed from you—the size of the backswing provides enough force to get the job done. You can use this shot for various distances by simply changing the size of the backswing.

Using the Putter for Approach Shots

If the ball is resting on the first cut around the green (the apron) or on the fairway within 15 feet from the edge of the green, the putter is an excellent club selection. It is the easiest club to use because no one is trying to get the ball up with a putter, so the lifting attitude, which causes so much difficulty in the short game, is eliminated.

To make a successful shot with the putter, the area over which the ball is to roll has to be very smooth, and the grass rather short.

The stroke is the same as if the ball were on the green, and the grip can be that of your putting stroke or the same as you use for regular shots.

As in any other shot, practice is the key. Through practice you will learn the influence of the longer grass on the roll of the ball. Because of the proximity of the ball to the edge of the green, the influence of the grass on the shot will not be as great as it may appear.

Getting the Ball to Stop Close to the Target

On a level green, the target is the hole. On a sloping green the target is that point even with the hole to which the ball is directed.

Before you execute a pitch shot or chip shot, you must have a very clear picture of where the target is located and at the same time visualize the ball stopping at the target. This is the same mental concern that must exist while putting.

Regardless of how much sense all this makes, the secret to success is practice, practice, and more practice.

Chapter 8

Putting

Being a good putter entails doing some very important things to perfection.

1. Reading the green.

   a. Reading the speed.

   b. Reading the break—the amount of slope that is going to control how the putt rolls.

   c. Reading the grain—the direction in which the grass grows.

2. Placing the putter face at a right angle to the line selected.

3. Rolling the ball on the line selected.

4. Imparting to the ball sufficient speed to reach the target.

   a. The target is the hole if the putt is straight.

   b. The target is a point even with the hole to which the ball is being directed in a putt that will break either to the right or to the left.

The Putting Grip

Putting grips vary a great deal more than the grip for normal golf shots.

- A common grip is the reverse overlap, which means that all of the fingers of the low hand are on the shaft of the putter and the index finger of the high hand is over the fingers of the low hand. See Figure 31.

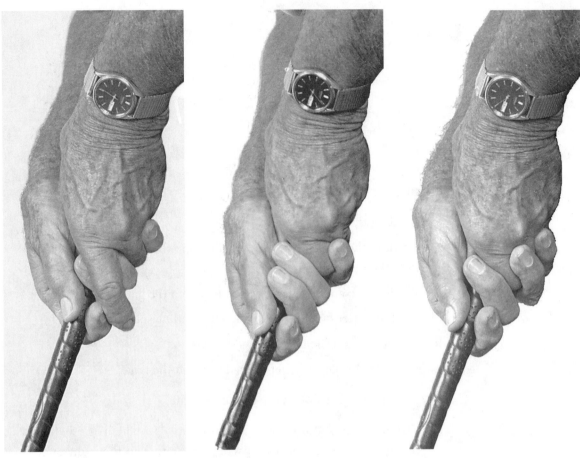

| *Figure 31* | *Figure 32* | *Figure 33* |

- Another type is the normal golf grip, which is the regular grip with a single overlap where the little finger of the low hand rests on top of the index finger of the high hand. See Figure 32. A variation of this grip is the double overlap, where two fingers of the low hand rest over the fingers of the high hand. See Figure 33.

- In the cross handed grip, the low hand in the normal grip becomes the high hand and the high hand becomes the low hand. This is becoming a fairly popular grip.

Figure 34

- In the ten finger grip, all fingers of both hands are in contact with the putter shaft. The hands can be together or can be slightly apart.

- For players using a long putter, the high hand is at the end of the shaft and is held close to the chest, while the low hand is placed down the shaft with the arm fully extended. See Figure 34.

If the putter has a very flat lie, the grip can be the same as it is on a regular shot, but as the putters become more upright and the player is closer to the ball, the hands turn out slightly so that the palms turn more toward the ball. The shaft of the putter then will run more up and down in the hands rather than across.

Because putting success is so dependent on individual feel, no grip is recommended. All players who use any of above grips can and do putt very well. What is important is that your hands be balanced, so that one hand does not work against the other and change the clubface direction when the putter is in motion.

Regardless of the grip used, the grip pressure must remain constant throughout the stroke—this will create a constant stroke.

Putting Stance and Address Position

With putting stance and address position, individuality again has to be respected. Some players prefer to place the ball off their front foot, others prefer to place it toward the back foot, and still others prefer to place the ball so that when taking the stance, the putter is in the center of the stance.

I start everyone with the ball placed so that the putter is in the center of the stance. As players develop, they may change that position. However, a player who has the putter in a position other than centered must follow this rule: If the putter is in the center of the stance, the weight is equally distributed on the feet. If the putter is not in the center of the stance, the weight must not remain equal.

Regardless of the position of the putter, toward the front or back foot, if the putter is placed at the midpoint between the shoulders and allowed to hang vertically, the head of the putter should fall exactly behind the ball. This means that if the ball is placed toward the front foot, the weight will be shifted to the front foot and must remain there. Should the player prefer to place the ball toward the back foot, the same test can be used and again the putter head must fall exactly behind the ball—the weight will be shifted toward the back foot and must remain there.

The reason for this change in weight location is the need to have the shoulders in the same plane as the line on which the ball is to be rolled. If the ball is placed toward the front foot and the weight remains equal on the feet, the shoulders will line up in the direction of the side the front foot is to the player. The same will hold if the ball is placed toward the back foot. This means the following: If the ball is placed toward the front foot (the left foot of the right-handed player), the shoulders will line up to the left. If the ball is placed toward the back foot (the right foot), the shoulders will line up to the right. Both right- and left-handed players can use this type of reasoning.

If the weight remains equal but the ball is placed toward the front foot, the putter shaft will be at a slant and the clubhead will be ahead of the end of the shaft. The opposite will hold if the ball is placed toward the back foot—the clubhead will be behind the end of the shaft. By making the weight adjustment, the shaft of the putter will be straight up and down when looking at the player from the front.

It is much easier to line up the face of the putter in the direction in which the ball is to be sent if the shaft is straight up and down. If the clubhead is ahead of the end of the shaft, the face of the putter will be aiming in the direction of the front foot. If the clubhead is behind the end of the shaft, the face of the putter will be aiming in the direction of the back foot. To change these normal reactions, the player would have to open or close the face of the putter, making the rolling of the ball in the desired direction rather difficult.

Warning: If you have learned to putt with your putter in the center of the stance and you find that you prefer to putt with the putter toward the front foot, when you adjust your weight distribution, be sure that you shift your weight in a lateral direction. Do not face the new club placement. If you do, the putter face will be aiming to the left for right-handed players and to the right for left-handed players. The opposite will be true if the body faces the back foot.

The Address

The address position is taken in the same manner as it is taken for any other shot. Keep your eyes on the point to which you are going to direct the ball and then place the putter face at a right angle to that line. Once that has been done, your body should be squared with the putter face whether it is toward the front or back foot or in the center of the stance.

Practice Exercise

There are times when all of us lose the right angle perception, and then it is difficult to place the face of the putter in the direction the ball has to roll. What can be done under these circumstances? The old adage of four eyes are better than two is one solution. Ask someone to check and if he or she says that the line you took is incorrect, then have that person hold the putter so you can check the alignment. Seeing is believing. This check determines what the problem is, but how can you fix it? I recommend putting down a mirror 1 foot wide by 3 feet long, which has two strips of 1/4-inch black tape running down the center the long way, very close to each other and yet far enough apart to create a very narrow path for the ball to roll on. About 12 inches from one end, place another piece of tape at 90 degrees to the long pieces and use this to place the putter face. See Figure 35. This will

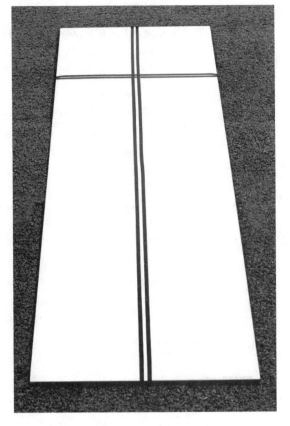

Figure 35

show you the right angle between the putter face and the path on which the ball is to be rolled. When the ball is rolled on the mirror, the goal is to keep it between the two long strips of black tape. See Figures 36 and 37.

Another way to check alignment is to use a putter that remains standing when you remove your hands from it. Using this type of putter, take your address position in the normal way, remove your hands from the putter, and then go behind it and check to see if the face of the putter is lined up on the line selected. This will show whether you have a tendency to aim to the right or left.

Maintain great flexibility in the arms and the next step is the stroke.

The Putting Stroke

Basically speaking, the putting stroke is just a small swinging motion, it does not differ from the swing used with the driver or any of the other golf clubs. Years ago the putting stroke was made with a very low center while today it is made with a very high center. What does this mean? Most of the good putters on the tour when I used to play the Winter tour used a low-center stroke, they were "hand" putters. If you use your hands to produce a putting stroke, there is a lot of activity in the wrists. Today's good putters use a high center, which means that they use their arms to produce the stroke—they use their arms both in the backswing and the forward swing, and wrist activity is greatly diminished.

Figure 36

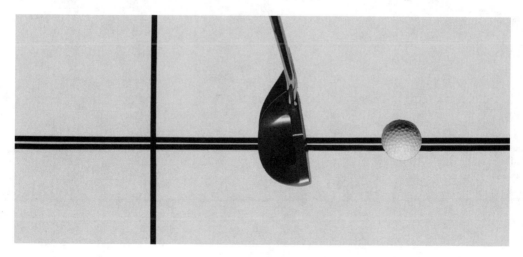

Figure 37

Some great putters used their hands to putt, but the quality of the stroke of today's great putters is outstanding because, by using the arms to putt, the inconsistencies inherent in a hand stroke are eliminated. There is very little wrist activity, and in many cases none at all. This lack of hand use, just as in the full shots produces great consistency.

Practice Exercise

To get a good understanding of a high-center stroke, take a putter and place the end of the shaft against your body, extend your arms and grip the putter down the shaft toward the head. Now move the putter back and forth, keeping the end of the shaft against your body. See Figures 38, 39, and 40. The only possible way to do this is with your arms. If your hands get involved, the end of the shaft will change location, it will not remain in

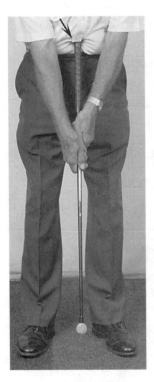

Figure 38

Figure 39

Figure 40

the same place it was when you gripped the putter. This is a stroke produced with a high center.

If you were to roll a ball on the ground to a certain point, you would use your arm to do it, you would not flip your hand and leave your arm motionless. The putting motion is the same.

Here are two excellent thoughts that produce good putts:

- Swing the putter back and forth with the arms.

- Focus on the putter: Swing both ends of the putter back and forth together.

How Is the Putter Swung?

Should the putter be swung straight back and straight forward? My answer is No. The golf swing is circular in shape whether it is produced with a driver or a putter. The only way a putter can be swung straight back and forward is if it is held vertically as the pendulum of a clock. No putter that I have ever seen has been manufactured to be perfectly vertical to the ground at the address position, it is always inclined to it. With the shaft in this inclined position, when the putter is put in motion, it moves in a circular pattern. The greater the inclination (the flatter the putter is), the more pronounced the circular pattern.

As far as the face of the putter is concerned, the more inclined the shaft, the more the face fans out. If the shaft were perfectly vertical, then the face would remain at a right angle (square) to the putting line.

If a player attempts to keep the face of the putter square to the putting line with a putter whose shaft is not vertical, the face would have to be closed in the backswing and opened in the forward swing. Not very easy to keep the stroke consistent when the putter has to be manipulated constantly.

If you hold your hand out in front of you with the arm at any angle, and you slapped it with the other hand, the slapping hand would not go straight back and palm down and then go straight forward with the palm up. Watch closely and you will see that it fans out naturally and moves in a circular pattern making it very easy to slap your stationary hand. This is the normal motion and the putter should move the same way.

Body Motion

Body motion in putting is quite different from the rest of the game. The movement is so small that there is no need for much body activity. From the hips down there should be absolutely no motion, as though that part of your body were frozen. The putter swings from the shoulders and what little body motion there is takes place in the upper torso. It's as though the arms are hanging from the shoulder joints and they swing from those joints. The shoulders will have some motion, but it will be in relation to the plane of the putter swing.

Too many putts are missed because the upper torso is turned toward the hole, causing putts to be missed to the right or left of the hole. When we have short putts, there is a great tendency to do this. We seem to turn to the hole prematurely as though we are ready to get the ball out of the hole before it gets there. I like to feel that when I strike a putt, I am always facing the ball or where it was before being struck. To accomplish this, you want to see the spot where the ball was resting appear after the ball is struck. As soon as it appears, you can follow the ball. Waiting to see the spot where the ball was resting keeps your body very quiet and prevents changing the direction of your stroke.

Stroke Size

How big should the stroke be? In my understanding of the physics of the golf swing, the size of the stroke must be directly proportional to the distance the ball is to be sent. The longer the distance the larger the stroke, the shorter the distance the smaller the stroke. I disagree with the theory that the backswing should be small and the follow-through long. When the backswing is made smaller than is required for the distance to the target, it makes the player use a hitting action to send the ball to its destination. The problem with this idea is that players who use it tend to make a similar size backswing whether the ball has to go 6 feet or 60 feet.

If a ball is thrown to a particular destination 6 feet away, the person throwing it will not make the same size movement with his arm as if the ball were thrown 60 feet away. The interesting thing is that when throwing a ball we give no thought to the size of the arm movement, it is simply left to instinct. The same should occur in our putting stroke. Through practice we learn how much force a swing produces, not as a backswing or a forward swing, but as a whole. The size and force are not controlled consciously but by sensing the force generated by the swinging motion.

Sometimes when I play in a group, and one person is ready to putt, a well-meaning friend will say, "remember it's uphill." This sometimes influences the person putting to deliver a strong hit to the ball, which then goes well beyond the hole. Consciously trying to determine how hard to hit the ball is not the answer. If the friends were just walking up the hill, would one say, "remember it is uphill." No mention would be made and the friend would have no problem walking up the hill. The same instinct works when putting: If you look at the conditions, you will know it is uphill, no one has to tell you. This ability to determine conditions depends on your ability to read the green and it comes from practice and experience.

Reading the Green

Reading the green means determining whether the green is slow, medium, or fast. It is determining how much the slope on the putting line is going to affect the ball as it rolls to its destination. It is determining if there is grain on the green, which will change the speed of the green depending on whether the ball is rolling with the grain, against it, or across it. Teaching the procedure for reading greens is difficult because our eyes do not always see the same things and everyone does not strike the ball with the same force. These two things change the way we read greens.

Before talking about reading greens, we need to mention the two ways of putting: lag putting and aggressive putting.

Lag Putting

A lag putter putts so that the ball reaches the ball rolling slowly and stops very near the hole. The ball in lag putting is struck lightly. Lag putters will putt well on fast greens and slow greens. I have always been a lag putter. When my father taught me to putt, he used to tell me the following. "Let the ball reach the hole, stop, and look down in the hole and have it say, gee it looks nice down there, I think I will jump in." The beauty of this way of putting is that if the ball catches the rim of the hole, it has a chance to drop. Sometimes it can go all around the hole and still drop in.

Aggressive Putting

The second way to putt is to be an aggressive putter. Aggressive putters strike the ball quite hard for the distance the ball has to travel. The problem I see with this type of putting is that if the ball misses the hole it leaves too long a putt for the next putt. In short putts the ball has to hit the hole dead center in order to stay in, if it catches the rim, it will spin out and may leave the player with a longer putt than the preceding one.

If a lag putter fears leaving the ball short of the hole, a point 6 or 8 inches beyond the hole can be used as the target, and the ball can be lagged to that point. With the ball stopping 6 inches beyond the hole, the next stroke is merely a tap in, and the possibility of being short is eliminated.

On very fast greens aggressive putters have difficult times, leaving themselves much too long putts for their second putts. On these types of greens the lag putters get better results. If on these types of greens, besides being very fast they are very rolling, the lag putter will fare better. Aggressive putters fare better on slow greens than they do on fast greens.

Reading the Break

When playing a breaking putt:

- A ball will break more the faster the green is.
- A ball will break less the slower the green is.

- A ball will break more for the lag putter.

- A ball will break less for the aggressive putter.

What you have just read is the reason why it is difficult to teach players to read greens. Articles are written telling us the secrets of reading greens and I have tried them, but after all the reading and experimenting with those ideas, I go back to my original statement that one learns to read greens through experience, through practice. To learn well it is best to practice long breaking putts rather than short straight ones. The information gathered from this practice must then be used in order to putt the greens well when on the golf course.

Reading greens is so important. You can have a perfect stroke and send the ball exactly where you intended it to go, but if that is the wrong place because of improper reading, the ball will never go in the hole. There are days when all of us who play golf read so well that all our putts go in, and the next day nothing goes in. When they do not go in, without question we blame our stroke, so we go to the practice putting green and attempt to change our stroke. The stroke is never lost between rounds any more than the swing is lost between rounds or between shots or holes. A putt is missed, and seldom is "I misread the putt," given the blame.

Straight Line Putting and Curve Putting

Players have two methods to use when dealing with breaking putts. In the straight line method, the player estimates how many inches or feet the slope of the green is going to affect the roll of the ball. Then a spot even with the hole and at a distance from the hole that equals the estimated slope effect is picked and the ball is sent straight to that spot. The slope of the green will curve the ball to the hole. The player who uses this method only sees a straight line going to his target.

In the curve line method, the player actually sees the ball rolling on the curve to the hole. In some cases the player actually determines at what point on the curve the ball will start curving the most. This player never sees straight lines.

Should You Concentrate on Making Putts

I recommend that players do not concentrate on making putts or on putting the ball in the hole.

When my daughter Lynn was about four years old I took her to the putting green at the Milwaukee Country Club with one of our junior putters and I said to her. "Lynn, put the ball in the hole." She looked at me and without hesitation, picked up the ball, walked to the hole and put it in the hole. Unfortunately, the rules of the game of golf do not permit us to do that. It would be wonderful if we could, just think of how many times we would shoot in the 60s or 70s.

The ball dropping in the hole is the result of doing three things well. First, the setup or address position must be correct, and then there are only two more things left to do, nothing more.

1. To roll the ball on the correct line and

2. To give it the proper speed to get there.

If we do these two things, the ball will go into the hole without any further influence from us. It matters not whether the putt is 2 feet long or 40 feet long, what we have to do never changes.

How do we give the correct speed to the ball so it stops where it has to? We have to do the same thing we do when we throw a ball to someone. The first thing we do is to look at whom we are going to throw the ball, we never take our eyes off that person, and then we send the ball directly to that person.

So in putting, and for that matter in every shot we make, we have to see the target. This does not mean that we look at it when taking our position at the ball and then forget about it. After all, when playing golf we do not look at our target, we look at the ball, so how can we see the target? Very easily. The moment our eyes pick up the target, a picture is created in our mind. In putting it is the hole in a straight putt or a point above the hole in a breaking putt.

We must hold that picture in our mind's eye while making the stroke. The location of the target must be clearly seen in our mind while making the stroke or we do not have a place to send the ball.

Through this visualization of the location of the target, our mind computes two things:

- The size of the stroke.

- The force necessary to get the ball to the target. Unfortunately I find too many individuals attempting to determine how big a swing they must make and how hard to hit the putt. Neither one of these two concerns can be determined. Putting is based on the feel of the distance that our eyes transmit to our mind, and to a certain extent it depends on how we feel on a particular day. Because of this human element that makes us so variable, the putting stroke will differ from day to day, and this cannot be controlled consciously. Some days it will be larger than other days, and some days smaller.

If we were to putt just one ball from a distance of 20 feet on a fairly rolling surface every day for one month, some days we would tend to go beyond the hole, some days we would tend to be short, and some days the distance would be perfect. The same thing happens with the break—some days our eyes will see more break than other days. This is the price we pay for being human beings and not machines. And this is why some days every ball we strike on the green goes in the hole and other days the hole seems to move as our ball approaches it. The best thought, which overcomes a great deal of this human variability, is the thought I recommend to all players:

I will roll the ball on the line I have selected and visualize it stopping at the hole or at the spot to which I have decided to send it. In order to do this, my mind must hold a mental picture of the hole or the spot while making my stroke.

When we are concerned with making the putt, we put too much pressure on the result. By using the thought above, pressure disappears. It is a very easy way to remain relaxed, and being relaxed enhances touch and feel, which are so important in becoming a good putter.

The Yips

The yips to which so many players succumb is nothing more than the fear of missing a putt and the player's effort to force the ball to go into the hole, the desire to make the putt. A yip action is always produced with the hands and it is a very sudden motion. If the desire to make the putt is eliminated and the putter is swung with the arms, it is practically impossible to fall prey to the yips.

Remember that making a putt is the result of having read the green correctly first of all. Then just send the ball in the direction you have decided upon from reading the green with enough force to get to the target you want to reach. By doing these three things without any intent of making the putt while executing the putting stroke, the ball will drop into the hole.

Chapter 9

Playing the Unusual Shots

This chapter is devoted to playing shots from lies where the ground is not level. For the reader to understand the procedures for making these shots, the reader needs to know my definition of each of these lies. When facing the ball:

- A sidehill lie is one where the hill is rising to the left or right of the player.

- An uphill lie is one where the hill rises in front of the player. The ball rests higher than the player's feet.

- A downhill lie is one where the hill descends in front of the player. The ball is lower than the player's feet.

The secret to success in playing from these lies is the manner in which the player sets up, the address position. The sidehill lies require more adjustments than either the uphill or downhill lies. The ball position has to be changed in order to fit the inclination of the slope, and the equal weight balance on the feet for level lies must also be changed.

Sidehill Lies

The Hill Descending Toward the Low (Front) Foot

The ball is placed toward your high (back) foot, the weight is on your low foot and remains there while swinging. See Figure 41. The steeper the hill, the farther toward your high foot the ball should be. Your body is tilted to fit the hill and stays in that tilted attitude when swinging, so that it is possible to swing with the hill. See Figure 42. When the shot is played correctly, it will feel to you that, after the clubhead meets the golf ball, the clubhead continues on the grass down the hill. If your body, as soon as the swing is started, reverts to the position it would have on a level lie, the clubhead will strike the ground well behind the ball. The right foot is the high foot and the left foot is the low foot.

Because the ball is placed toward the back foot, the shot will have a much lower trajectory, so select a higher number club for this shot. Woods should not be used from this type of sidehill lie.

Figure 41

Figure 42

On this sidehill lie, the ball will have a tendency to go to the right, so to send the ball straight, place the clubhead behind the ball at a right angle to the target line. This delofts the clubhead so the shot will be even lower.

If it is necessary to get some height on the shot, instead of placing the clubhead at a right angle to the target line at address, place it fanned out. When the clubhead is fanned out, it will be facing to the right but will retain its normal loft—it is actually out of square to the target line. With the clubhead in this position, not only will the ball start to the right but will have a tendency to slice so it will be necessary for you to be aligned even more to the left in order to be able to send the ball toward the target.

The Hill Ascending Toward the High (Front) Foot

The ball is placed toward your high foot, the weight is on your low (back) foot and remains there while swinging. See Figure 43. The steeper the hill, the farther toward your high foot the ball should be. Your body is tilted to fit the hill and stays in that tilted attitude when swinging, so that it is possible to swing with the hill. When the shot is played correctly, it will feel to you that after the clubhead meets the golf ball the clubhead continues on the grass up the hill. If your body, as soon as the swing is started, reverts to the position it would have on a level lie, the clubhead will get embedded into the hill, it will not be possible to finish over the shoulder. (In this type of lie the high foot is the left foot and the low foot is the right foot for right-handed players. For left-handed players it is the reverse.)

This shot will be much higher than normal and will have a tendency to go to the left. You should set your alignment to the right of the target to allow for this tendency. For these shots a lower number club should be used.

Uphill Lie

When facing an uphill lie, with the ball above your feet, the address position with regards to the ball and clubhead positions is the same as if it were a level lie. Place the club in the center of your stance. However, because of the hill, your body will be in a more erect position. It is advisable to grip down on the club so that you can be nearer the ball; by doing this the steepness of the hill is lessened. See Figure 44. The swing from this lie will have a flatter plane.

Expect the ball to be struck with a hooking spin making it go to the left. Set your alignment to the right of the target to allow for this type of ball flight.

Figure 43   *Figure 44*

If you want to lessen the tendency for the ball to be struck with a hooking spin, you can use one of these two procedures.

1. At the address position, instead of placing the clubhead square to the target line, you can place it slightly open. As you swing the club with the open blade, it will cancel out the hooking spin. Remember that when a clubhead is opened, it will hit the ball higher and lose some of its distance, therefore use a lower number club. The amount the clubhead is opened will differ for each player, so this procedure should be practiced to determine the proper amount to open the clubhead. The steeper the hill, the more it should be opened.

2. When taking the address position, place the ball toward the back foot and place the clubhead behind the ball in a fanned position, which will now be facing to the right (left for left-handed players). The alignment must be adjusted slightly to the opposite side of the target from where the clubface is aiming. This will impart a slicing spin to the ball, which will cancel the hooking spin caused by the uphill lie. This is the same setup used when setting up in a sand bunker to play a fairway bunker shot. Let's review it. Take a normal address position at a spot about 2 inches to the target side of the ball, then move the clubhead behind the ball without moving anything else. When you make the swing, the club is swung at the spot that was addressed prior to placing the clubhead behind the ball.

Downhill Lie

In the downhill lie, the ball lies below your feet. Take the normal address position with the club in the center of your stance, weight equally distributed on your feet. The effect:

1. This position is rather uncomfortable, especially if the slope is rather steep. To be able to place the clubhead at the ball, your body has to have an excessive forward bend.

2. The weight has a tendency to be forced toward your toes because of the slope.

3. The ball will have a tendency to go to the right (left for left-handed players).

Because of the excessive bend of your body, swinging to the end of the backswing is somewhat uncomfortable, so when you swing the club there is a tendency to straighten your body to the normal position of a level lie. Making the swing from that more erect position results in the clubhead being too high above the ball, so you top the ball.

To eliminate this problem, widen your stance in order to lower the center (the midpoint between your shoulders). See Figure 45. This makes it easier to reach the ball. With this wider stance you can produce good shots, but:

1. Your body as well as your swing will be somewhat restricted.

2. Because of this re- striction, your shots will be a bit shorter. A longer club should be used.

If points 1 and 2 are accepted, you will have no difficulty producing good shots. The ball posi- tion is the same in this type of lie as it is in the level lie. There is no need to change the clubhead position unless you wish to cancel the tendency of the ball to go to the right (left for left-handed play-

Figure 45

ers), in which case the clubhead should be placed slightly closed at the address.

Remembering Ball Direction from Non-level Lies

Here is an easy way to remember ball direction from sidehill, uphill, and downhill lies.

For Sidehill Lies

The ball will be directed in the direction of the foot toward which the ball is placed. If it is placed toward the left foot, it will tend to go left. If it is placed toward the right foot, it will tend to go right.

For Uphill and Downhill Lies

The ball will be directed in the same direction as it would go if it were putted.

If Low Shots are Needed

1. If the reason for the low shot is that you are playing into the wind, playing a less lofted club is your best alternative. It is imperative to keep a mental picture of the target so that the size of your swing will fit the distance the ball has to be sent.

2. If a low shot is the option you select, a less lofted club is a good decision. However, lowering the trajectory of a golf shot can also be done by moving the ball back in your stance with any club. Be aware though that lower shots always have less distance.

3. If the position of the ball is such that branches from a tree are in the path of the ball flight and located 30 yards or more from the ball, the best club to use is the driver gripped short and using what would feel like a three-quarter swing. Almost any other club will raise the ball too quickly and hit the branches, which could produce a worse situation. The important thing to do in this situation is to get the ball past the

branches—distance is not the top priority. If the tree branches were closer, other clubs could be used and the matter of distance could then be a consideration.

If Higher Shots Than Normal Are Necessary

When lower shots are necessary, a less lofted club can be used because the distance needed is less than the distance the club can produce. However, if full shots are necessary and more height is needed, taking a more lofted club will decrease the distance so that is not the thing to do. If, for example, you are using a 5-iron but greater height than usual is needed, the ball should be placed slightly forward in your stance (more to your front foot). However, to be successful, when taking your stance and addressing the ball, take an address position as though the ball were located about 2 inches back of where it really is, and that is where the club is swung. Do not place the clubhead at the ball, start from the position 2 inches behind the ball and make your normal swing, do not change the intent to the ball. Should the intent revert to the ball, the shot will not have the extra height.

When playing less than full shots, the same procedure can be used, but there is another alternative, which is to use a more lofted club and allow the extra loft of the club to produce the extra height. *You should never manipulate the clubhead to increase the height of the shots.*

Intentional Hooks and Slices

My belief is that no matter what type of ball flight is desired, the golf swing should not be changed. The club should be allowed to change the ball flight rather than the club's swing. For a right-handed player a hooked shot is produced by the club striking the ball and imparting a counterclockwise spin to it. The ball curves to the left. A counterclockwise spin will produce a slicing shot for the left-handed player.

For a right-handed player a sliced shot is produced by the club striking the ball and imparting a clockwise spin to it. The ball curves to the right. A clockwise spin will produce a hooking shot for the left-handed player.

Hooks

If you want a hooking flight, your address position should be the same as if the ball were to be sent straight, with the following exceptions:

1. Close the clubface to whatever degree the ball is to be hooked.

2. The clubface must be facing the direction in which the ball is to start. If the closed clubface is facing the target where you want the ball to end, as the ball curves it will move away from the target instead of toward it.

3. Your body should be positioned so that it faces the shaft of the club squarely, which will set the body farther to the opposite side of where the ball is to end.

After this setup has been accomplished, make your swing the same way as if the ball were to be sent straight. The clubface will impart the spin to the ball. Remember that when the clubface is closed, it will be somewhat de-lofted, producing lower than normal shots. To get higher shots, use a higher number club, or the ball should be placed slightly toward your front foot.

If you want a low hook, the ball should be placed slightly toward the back foot or lower number clubs should be used—no other changes are necessary.

Slices

If you want a slicing flight, your address position should be the same is if the ball were to be sent straight, with the following exceptions:

1. Open the clubface to whatever degree the ball is to be sliced.

2. The clubface must be facing the direction in which the ball is to start. If the open clubface is facing the target where you want the ball to end, as the ball curves it will move away from the target instead of toward it.

3. Your body should be positioned so that it faces the shaft of the club squarely, which will set the body farther to the opposite side of where the ball is to end.

After this setup has been accomplished, make your swing the same way as if the ball were to be sent straight. The clubface will impart the spin to the ball. Remember that when the clubface is open, it will have greater loft, producing higher shots than normal.

If the extra height is not desired, the setup should be taken as though a fairway bunker shot were to be played. Take your normal address position at a spot about 2 inches in front of the ball, and then just move the clubhead behind the ball in a fanned position.

This fanned position will not give the shot extra height. Swing the club at the spot that was addressed prior to moving the clubhead behind the ball.

The swing should be your normal swing, nothing should be changed. The clubface will impart the spin to the ball.

I want to remind the reader that you can play all sorts of shots while using the same swinging motion. If you practice these unusual shots for any length of time to become proficient, it will not affect your ability to hit the straight shots whenever you like. But think of the difficulty you would have if you had to change your swing in a different way for each of the special shots. What a difficult time you would have if you wanted to hit the ball straight after working on the special shots for a period of time.

Let the golf club give you the types of shots you desire while never changing your golf swing.

Playing Shots From the Rough

I maintain that even though the ball may be resting in the rough, the address position and the swing should be exactly the same as if the ball were resting in the fairway. I do not like to place the ball to my back foot because this causes the shot to come out very low, and that is not what is needed from the rough. Let's look at the ball surrounded by grass.

Ball Surrounded by Grass

When the ball is surrounded by grass, the important things are:

- Making a wise club selection.

- Accepting the fact that the shot will have less distance.

- Realizing that because there will be a great deal of grass between the ball and the clubface, the ball will roll a great deal more after it lands.

- Expecting that some shots from the rough will have a tendency to fly out of control. These are referred to as flyers.

Wise club selection can turn an apparently difficult shot into a fairly easy one. Clubs with more loft usually produce better results because the loft makes the ball rise and sends it through the upper part of the grass, which is fairly loose. If a club such as a 3-iron is selected, it will send the ball quite low and through that part of the grass that is rather thick and packed—the ball will not get a chance to get into the air. A 6- or 7-iron will give you greater distance and will take away the desire to strike the ball with great force.

Accepting the lack of distance allows you to maintain the freedom of your normal swing, which produces better quality shots and better distance than if you try for distance. No one likes to be in the rough, but everyone at one time or another will be there, and accepting the penalty for such a lie may result in not losing any strokes. We must use common sense in difficult situations—it always pays off.

I see so many players using so much effort to get the ball out of the rough. All that effort is wasted. To get good results, speed is necessary and the best way to be sure that speed is attainable is to remain as flexible as possible. The more effortless the swing is, the greater the possible speed, even in the rough.

Accepting the fact that there will be a great deal of grass between the ball and the clubface makes us choose different types of shots and affects our club selection. If we are playing a pitch shot to the green from the rough, with no hazards to carry, instead of landing the ball on the green and having it roll excessively, landing the ball short of the green and using the grass on the fairway to slow down the roll of the ball may be the best way to go. This is part of evaluating the circumstances and conditions and fitting the game to those circumstances and conditions to obtain the best results possible.

The flyers are rather unpredictable—sometimes they occur and sometimes even if the conditions seem to indicate that they would occur, they do not. So, it is difficult to prepare for them. If the ball reacts and you do not plan for it, the shot will go too far. If the ball does not react and you plan for it, then the shot will fall short of the intended target.

Ball On Top of Grass

If the ball is in the rough but is resting on top of the grass, you can use any club depending on the distance needed or desired. However, if the rough is very high and the ball is resting on top of it, do not ground your club. If you do, it is probable that the clubhead will slide under the ball and never move it. The ball will just drop into the divot. The other possibility is to pop the ball straight up in the air. For this situation, place the clubhead even with the ball.

Part V

Beyond the Swing

Chapter 10

Power

If golfers could play the game of golf without concern for this word power, everyone could improve his or her game at least 50%. For so many individuals power is the destroyer of their swing and thus their golf game. Why is power such an all-consuming attitude? Why isn't our attention placed on straightness or accuracy? The culprit, of course, is the human element. All golfers seem to think they are as strong or stronger than anybody, and that they should send the golf ball equally as far or farther than their buddies.

There seems to be so much more pride in being 300 yards from the tee than in being 1 inch from the hole after a shot needing a short iron. The game of golf is a target game—it does a player no good to hit the ball 300 yards and send it into heavy rough, into a grove of trees, or out of bounds.

In discussing the development of power, two words need clarification.

One is acceleration, the other is speed. They are not synonymous. Speed is the result of acceleration. When acceleration is constant, speed increases. When speed is constant, acceleration is zero.

To achieve the greatest speed within your potential, the highest rate of acceleration within your potential must be used. This rate is different whenever we play. It varies from individual to individual, it varies from day to day, and it can even vary within the same 18-hole round. Of course, we do not consciously vary our acceleration, it is simply a matter of being. The important thing is that whatever our acceleration is, as established by our current state, it is never changed during the swinging motion.

Acceleration—How Is the Propelling Force Created?

How do we apply power within the swinging motion? As mentioned before, given a certain size arc, the swinging motion produces the greatest amount of force that can be produced within that arc. The basis of developing speed in the golf swing is the same as it is when driving a car, throwing a ball, swinging a baseball bat—simply acceleration. The word acceleration in itself implies constancy of action and purpose.

Acceleration is a constant increase of speed per unit of time or space.

Where do we start to accelerate the club in order to obtain maximum speed at ball contact? The moment we start the forward swing is where, but remember this: Once the acceleration has been set at that point, it must never change prior to contact with the ball.

Before proceeding further, let us look at some very important characteristics of a swing.

Practice Exercise

Hold a golf club at the end of the shaft, vertically in front of you with the thumb and forefinger of either hand and swing it back and forth until it reaches a horizontal level on both sides. As you are doing this, observe:

1. The bottom (or lowest point) of the arc is the center of that arc.

2. The clubhead is moving at the greatest speed at the center of that arc.

3. The moment the club starts swinging from either horizontal level, it starts to accelerate and maintains that acceleration until it reaches the center of the arc—the point of greatest speed.

4. The instant the club passes that center point, it automatically starts to decelerate until it reaches the horizontal level and zero speed on the other side of center.

5. The acceleration and deceleration rates are exactly the same and constant.

6. The distances from the center of the arc to the horizontal levels on either side of the center are exactly the same. It is a symmetrical motion.

These six points contain the principles of a swinging motion with regard to speed. Given these points, when the acceleration is set at the beginning of our forward swing, it should be maintained until the clubhead reaches the midpoint of the arc. The midpoint of the forward swing is past the ball in a full swing. It is a fact that the speed of the clubhead is reduced by about 19% due to meeting the golf ball, which is a stationary object. However, we must retain our acceleration as though there were no resistance—*no ball*.

When playing shots that are less than full shots, our swings have more symmetry. The distance from the end of the backswing to the ball and from the ball to the end of the swing are very much the same. In this case the point of maximum speed will be at the moment of impact—the center of that arc. This is the case when we play three-quarter shots, half shots, pitch shots, chip shots, and putting.

Speed

For each arc size, there is a set speed. Within a certain arc, you cannot swing a club slower or faster than the size allows. If you try to increase or decrease the acceleration, the size of the arc will get larger or smaller respectively.

Since we swing the golf club from the end of the backswing to the end of the swing with our arms, when acceleration is applied, *it is applied with our arms*. Again be reminded that the arms are not the forearms.

If the speed is in our arms, everything that is moving will have speed. Any desire to add more speed as the club approaches the ball by throwing the clubhead with the intention of "hitting harder" will shift the responsibility for the forward swing from our arms to our body or hands. Once our hands or body take over, our arms will slow down and speed will be decreased. Bad shots will be the result, but it is very difficult to foresee the type of shots that will result from this type of acceleration change. It all depends on the degree of change, at what point we start to make the change, the type of action we use to make the change, and the suddenness with which we make the change.

You can clearly see that when the hands are used in the forward swing, topping, hooking, slicing, and shanking are all serious possibilities.

However if we increase the acceleration suddenly with our arms as the club reaches the ball, the reaction will not be as varied as when done with our hands. The following can still occur:

1. If we become rigid in our arms because of our effort to suddenly increase the acceleration, we could top the ball.

2. The ball could be caught very clean and very low on the clubface.

3. The ball will tend to slice if contacted on the face of the clubhead.

When an instructor tells a student to increase the speed of the forward swing, the student may have one or more interpretations.

1. He wants me to hit the ball farther.

2. More distance means I have to hit harder.

3. To hit harder, I must make the clubhead go faster.

4. In order to make the clubhead go faster, I must snap my wrists harder.

None of these four points is what the instructor meant when asking that the forward swing be made faster. What he or she meant is that the forward swing as a whole be made faster, not just at impact time. It is too late by then.

We should not differentiate what goes faster and when it goes faster. If the clubhead is to go faster, the shaft, the hands, the forearms, the arms, the shoulders, the body, the legs, and the footwork will all be faster if the acceleration is applied properly. Since our arms trigger the motion, they are also responsible for triggering the acceleration, and once they trigger it, everything mentioned in this paragraph goes right along with them.

When your arms set the acceleration, everything that will be moving must move in relation to that acceleration. If the acceleration is increased by 5%, every component part of the swing increases by that same percentage.

When the wish for greater distance is interpreted merely as creating greater speed, the swing will be very constant, very smooth, and will not get a chance to go astray.

By using the speed concept, if the player is already swinging at the highest potential, greater speed will not be possible, but the swing will not be damaged and cause bad shots as would happen if the idea of hitting the ball harder were used.

Relationship Between Strength and Speed

We might think that very strong people would send the ball farther than people of lesser strength, but it has been proven that this is not necessarily so. In order to send a golf ball a long way, the player has to be able to convert strength into speed. The greater this ability, the greater the distance.

It is not possible to send the ball a long ways just by using one's strength.

Should the Backswing Be Made Faster if the Forward Swing is Made Faster?

No, it should not. Regardless of the increase of the forward swing speed, the speed of the backswing should never be changed. The speed of the backswing has no influence on the forward swing speed. After all, the speed to send the ball can only be created in the forward swing.

Any increase in speed requires an increase in space. Thus, if you were to increase the speed of your backswing, the backswing would have to become longer to accommodate that increase. This increase in length is really not available to you, because once your golf swing has been formed, you give it a certain length that remains rather constant. If the speed is increased, you would stop the backswing at the normal length, but because the club is moving faster, you would have to stop the club with great effort. This extra effort would create great rigidity, the greatest enemy of an effortless flowing golf swing.

This discussion applies to a full swing. If you were making a less than full swing, you would still have some room to accommodate greater speed until the swing became full.

Summary: The acceleration of the golf club must be set at the beginning of your forward swing and maintained past the ball, with your body responding to that acceleration.

Advice: Determine what your distance potential is. Once this potential has been determined—play with it.

If you feel that your potential is still to be reached, attempt to reach it first by making a better swing and second by attempting to increase your arm speed.

A Final Word—Play to Your Own Potential

When playing golf with various individuals, golf professionals, low-handicap players, middle-handicap players, or high-handicap players, I find an interesting common denominator in their attitude toward distance. Most of these players miss their tee shots on the long yardage holes, be they par 3s, par 4s or par 5s.

Just because the scorecard shows 250-yard par 3s or 475-yard par 4s or 585-yard par 5s, these numbers do not make the players stronger. They remain the same players that on a previous hole hit a 60-yard shot with a wedge. Their strength or speed potential (distance potential) remains exactly the same. If the average tee shot for a player is 250 yards, regardless of what the scorecard says the length of the hole is, the average tee shot for that player remains the same.

When a player decides that more distance is necessary because of the yardage of the hole being played, that player will send the ball off line and will lose rather than gain distance.

May I repeat: When you determine your average distance potential while warming up prior to playing—Play with it or you may suffer serious and unpleasant consequences.

This applies whether your average tee shot is 125, 150, 175, 200, or 250 yards. The same attitude applies to every other shot regardless of type.

Chapter 11

The Mental Side

In this discussion of the mental side of golf, you should understand that whether or not your swing is in need of any corrections, the conclusions and recommendations of this discussion apply just the same.

Anytime golfers get together and discuss the game of golf, a common refrain is "Golf is all mental." No one has ever disagreed on the importance of mental attitude, yet when they go to the practice tee they work exclusively on the physical side of the game.

Who has ever heard a golfer say, "I am going to the practice tee to work on and improve my mental attitude." Indeed no one has. Our mind is what makes everything happen, so it is strange that we devote so little time and effort to making it work better. Clear thoughts, good concentration, and good mental direction will improve everyone's golf game.

Working on the mental phase of golf is not that difficult but requires strong self-discipline. Human beings are seldom willing to criticize themselves in terms of their own mental inefficiency.

It is difficult at times for an instructor to work on mental attitude with students. Many students, when they are told that their mental attitude and/or mental direction is incorrect, or that they are not thinking properly, think that they are being accused of lacking intelligence or mental capacity. Nothing could be further from the truth. These comments should be taken as important information worthy of consideration and improvement.

Everything we do in our lifetime is done with some sort of mental control—mental attitude. Golf is included in this "everything." What is the relationship between the mental and the physical sides of an activity? Without proper mental attitude, mental control, and mental direction (conscious or subconscious) there can be no physical performance.

Muscles do not move on their own; they need to be stimulated in order to move. They have no brain, no mind, so they cannot have any memory. They simply do what they are told to do through our mental processes. To produce a certain specific movement they must not only be stimulated for movement, but this stimulation must be directed so the muscles produce the movement desired. Without this direction, the movements produced will vary greatly and will most likely be incorrect for the desired result.

This direction and stimulation come from only one source—our mind. Many players in replaying their round tell of the shot they wanted to slice and came out with a hook and vice versa. Or the player who was under a tree had to play a low shot but hit the tree because the ball went high instead of low, in spite of the fact that his club selection was correct. These are examples of stimulation without direction.

If proper mental direction had been present, the players would never have achieved opposites of what they intended. Their degree of success might not have been 100% of what they planned, but it never would have come out as an opposite.

To have good mental attitude, we first of all need knowledge of what we must do in order to produce a movement with the club that will propel the golf ball toward the desired target. Once we know this, the next step is to believe in it, have faith in it, and trust it. Without this trust the desired results will never be achieved.

Players are constantly trying to develop a "grooved swing," but they will never develop a "grooved swing" unless they first "groove" their thoughts through mental discipline. In other words, they must "groove" the work of the mind, and this groove must be as narrow as possible and as deep as possible, so it becomes extremely difficult to slip out of it. Once we have established this deep groove, our mind will direct the same stimulus to the muscles over and over again, so that through familiarization it becomes easy for us to be repetitive in our action.

Needless to say, the player who never misses a shot has not been born and never will be born. We are human beings, not machines, and are susceptible to many stimuli, so if we miss a shot, we should realize that our mental direction was deficient. Our awareness of the proper swing was lost. So if we miss a shot, our concern in the next shot should be to regain the strength of our mental direction and pay close attention to only what is necessary.

Missed shots are part of the game of golf and the fact that we miss a shot now and then does not mean there is something wrong with our swing, that something has to be changed. If we are driving a car and come to an intersection where we should be turning left, but we turn right, would we say there is something wrong with the car?

We simply lost our mental purpose, acting without the proper mental direction.

Mental Attitudes

Mental attitudes can be grouped into three different categories:

- Positive
- Negative
- Corrective

A positive mental attitude is the one all golfers should cultivate because it concerns itself with what the person should do, without any concern with doubts or possible failures. Knowing what to do and having complete faith and trust in it brings about a strong positive mental attitude. The player should say: This is what I must do, when I do it, I get a perfect shot—my only concern is to execute it.

Players with a negative mental attitude always feel and expect bad shots from all the bad things that are thought to exist in the swing. The ball is going out of bounds or into the trees or into a water hazard or where yesterday the ball was unplayable. With this type of attitude, the player never sets a pattern to follow, and the results of the shots match the expectations, i.e., out of bounds, into the trees, into the water, or whatever else might have been in his or her mind. The player never has a plan of what must be done to achieve success, since the plan is to prevent something not desired from taking place.

In our daily activities no one makes a list at the beginning of the day of all the things we do not want to do. Someone going to buy groceries does not make a list of all the items not to be purchased. If we are driving to a certain destination, we do not make a list of the places we do not want to stop. In each of these examples we make a list of the items we want to purchase or the places we plan to stop. *We act in a positive way.*

With the corrective attitude the player is trying to constantly correct the swing in order to change the previous shot. Practically every time the player swings the club and hits a shot that does not go as intended, something wrong in the swing is blamed, so a change has to be made in the next swing to correct the next shot.

This player is constantly analyzing his or her swing in terms of what is wrong or what is thought to be missing in the swing. often the conclusion is simply a guess, so changes are made that have no bearing on the problem; so in the attempt to make a change through guesswork, another problem is created. The player has no real conception of what should be done with the golf club. As in the case of the negative attitude, consistency of performance is not possible since the player attempts something different every time the club is swung.

Maintaining Purpose

I hear so many times "I can do it on the practice tee but I cannot do it on the golf course" or "I can only do it when my instructor is with me." This is so common and it really is so sad. What causes this problem?

So many players hit a lot of practice balls and take lessons and their work is all wasted when on the golf course. They do not carry their improvement to the golf course. *The problem is a change in purpose.* When a golfer is working on the practice tee, that player is mentally concerned with his or her swing. Where the ball goes doesn't really matter very much because *there is no score* by which to be embarrassed.

However, when that same player goes to the golf course the concerns now are:

- Distance

- Score

- Where the ball goes or does not go

The mental attitude we develop on the practice and lesson tees must be taken to the golf course. *Perfect swings produce perfect shots.* If our swing is producing desirable shots on the practice and lesson tees, no matter where that swing is produced, it will produce the same desirable shots. *The golf course should not control the player.*

Everything we learn is learned with one purpose in mind—to perform it on the golf course so our scores will be what we wish them to be. There should be no change in mental attitude just because we are now on the golf course.

Mental Direction

We all have a great tendency to take for granted the success we achieve during a lesson or during a practice session. The idea that "I have it now" is the first step to disaster. When this happens there is a dangerous change in the player's mental attitude and mental direction. The player expects the swinging action will simply happen rather than be produced with a conscious awareness. I call this the *deterioration of the mental direction.* The player produces a motion with no direction from the mind to do it correctly. You don't "have it" unless you do it and know you did it.

No one, professional or amateur, can produce a swing through reflex and subconscious action alone and have it last. If this could be accomplished, touring professionals would never get off their games or miss shots and yet they do. In spite of the hours of practice and the rounds they play, their golf swing must be produced with good awareness and strong mental direction. When some of the great touring professionals make exceptional shots that result in winning or shooting a very low round and the sports writers ask them what was on their mind, the response is always the same, "I just wanted to put a good swing on it." We should all take that to heart.

If this mental concern is important for the tour player, imagine how important it is for the average player who sometimes goes for months without hitting a golf ball, or plays very few times a year, often does not warm up before going to the first tee, and most important of all does not practice enough to learn and have confidence in what the golf swing should be. Can the swing just happen under these conditions? Of course not.

The formula for taking the practice tee swing to the golf course is a simple one.

1. Know what your basic concept is.

2. Produce that concept through good mental direction.

3. Be aware that you are doing what you want to do with the golf club.

4. Work very hard to play the game on the golf course with the same mental attitude that you developed in the practice session.

5. The golf swing must remain the primary concern. *Remember that perfect swings produce perfect results.* The swing always takes place before the shot and no one can change this sequence.

If you know your swing, observe yourself, and remain aware of producing that swing, you will not allow any strange interferences to creep into your motion. You will have a very strong conscious mental direction.

A player who is not mentally aware of producing his or her desired swing and allows the motion to be a reaction will eventually allow strange things to creep into it, but unfortunately that player will not sense those changes. In a very short time the results of those unnoticed changes will bring failure to his or her game.

When my father and I had discussions about my game, even on the telephone, when we ended the discussion, his final words to me every time were *observe yourself*. He wanted me to be aware of what I was doing, in a very positive way.

All who play this wonderful game should develop this knack of observing themselves and seeing what has to be done to execute the desired good swing. If this observation is keen, all will reap great benefits.

Chapter 12

John Doe and His Game

This story shows a realistic pattern of play for many players. I am sure that a great number of readers will identify themselves with this John Doe.

John Doe contacts his golf professional to schedule a lesson. While working with the professional, he finds that sending the ball to his target in a very straight direction and with adequate distance is not at all difficult as long as he does what the instructor suggested. He listens well and understands exactly what he has to do. He is very pleased and vows to perfect what he has just learned. This is John Doe #1.

At a later time John Doe goes to the practice tee to work on the things he learned during the lesson with his instructor. He achieves the results he desires, but after a short period of time his results do not have the same quality they had at the beginning of the practice session. In trying to regain the good results he tries to figure out what he is not doing and proceeds to make changes, with the hope that he can bring things around. He is unsuccessful so he plans for another golf lesson. This is John Doe #2.

After his second lesson things improve and he feels that it's time to try it on the golf course. From the lesson tee, he goes to the first tee to play 9 holes, hoping to experience the success he had on the lesson tee.

His first tee shot happens to go slightly to the right of where he intended to send it. He plays another ball and this one goes to the left. He says to himself, "I don't understand, on the lesson tee I hit them all straight and I have hit two drives and neither one has gone straight."

When John Doe was on the lesson tee, taking his lesson, he didn't particularly care where the ball was going, he was working on accomplishing something with his swing as his instructor advised, and because it was sound, all his shots were straight. Now that he is on the golf course his concern is more with the result of the shot, so the correct swing is no longer of primary concern. This is John Doe #3.

After a few days of practice to attempt to do what his instructor told him to do, John Doe makes a game with his friends, who bring a fourth player, a stranger to John Doe, to complete the foursome. It turns out that the stranger is a fine player, not as good as John Doe but he achieves greater distance than John. As the game progresses, so does the decline of John Doe's game and he finds himself on the losing end. Well, this can't be, says John, I am going to beat this stranger, and he is going to find out that I can hit it as far as he can. Catastrophe has now set in and things go from bad to worse. Where has John's concept gone? It has been overshadowed by other concerns and what he learned about the swing from his instructor is no longer his concern. This is John Doe #4.

On a different day, John Doe has a game and one of his friends has asked the professional to complete the foursome, but John does not find out about this until he arrives at the club, has his practice, and goes to the first tee. When he finds out, he is concerned with trying to impress his instructor with his progress. Unfortunately this progress he is concerned with is based on how low he can score as proof of this progress. He is nervous: "What is my instructor going to say if I play badly!" His mind is a long way from where it should be. Where is the concern for the correct swing he experienced on the lesson and practice tees? He does not have it. This is John Doe #5

Then add to these situations a competition in a tournament, when the score is so important in everyone's mind, and again the concern for the swing goes a little further away. This is John Doe #6.

All these situations turn John Doe into a different person because his mental desires change with each one. No one can play well when one changes into all these different persons. If through a golf instructor you learn a sound concept that produces a sound repeating swing on the lesson and practice tees, would it not be reasonable to believe that no matter where it is produced it will also work? Certainly it would be more important to have this conviction on the golf course since only there does one count all the strokes taken. No one keeps a record of how many good or bad shots are made during the practice sessions.

Therefore, a player should remain John Doe #1 no matter what the circumstances of play, for only then does the player's purpose and concern remain the same.

Mental Direction and the Mental Lapse

How many times, we who have played golf for so long have missed a shot because of mental lapses instead of truly physical swing errors!

When this subject comes up in golf instruction, students are not as willing to accept the mental change as they are the physical change. If a player misses a shot and a physical cause is given for the miss, he will say "No wonder I missed it." He can quickly understand and accept that if the physical motion is incorrect, a good shot cannot be made.

However, if I tell the same player that the shot was missed because his basic thought was lost or changed, he will say that he didn't, that he was thinking of the same things as when he hit the good shots. Then, if asked what his thought was at the moment of impact or at the finish of the swing, he cannot say, he cannot remember. The player who misses a shot seldom, if ever, finds the cause in his mental failure at the time of execution.

We all agree that if a person has a swing that produces good shots most of the time, bad shots produced by the same person must have a faulty physical motion or action. The question is why was it faulty.

No swing will stay steady and consistent without the proper mental direction. If this mental direction is weak or disappears, the physical motion will show it. It would be too lengthy to cite all the causes of mental lapses or changed mental attitudes, but some examples will show what is meant.

On a certain day, Jane played the 9th hole at her club and sliced the ball out of bounds. The next day she is playing the 9th hole again and that out of bounds shot on the previous day makes her hit the shot with the idea of not going out of bounds. So she swings well to the left of the proper line and therefore slices more sharply than the previous day and she goes out of bounds again.

Jane should have been concerned with directing her swing with the proper principles in order to make the correct swinging motion in the direction of the target. Jane's mental direction was very poor—it was negative as well as corrective, though she would not admit that she was thinking of anything but to hit the ball down the fairway.

Regardless of what she says, her physical motion gave her away.

Another good example is what happens sometimes in putting. We leave the ball too short of or send it too far beyond the hole. We "forgot" where the hole was. We cannot get the ball to the hole if we forget its location or if our main concern is how big to make the swing or how hard to strike the golf ball. If those things are on our mind it is not possible to keep the hole's location in our mind as well.

Another example: On a breaking putt, the player takes the proper line and then in the middle of the stroke decides to play more or less break. Result: The putt is missed. Can we blame the stroke for the miss? Certainly not—there was a change in mental attitude and mental direction.

When playing well, too many players take their swing for granted and expect muscle memory to do the job. Muscle memory does not exist—muscles remember nothing since they have no brain. *When we depend on "muscle memory," our mind does not have much involvement, thus our swing has no mental direction.*

Swings not performing well because of mental lapses or mental changes cannot be corrected by making physical changes in the swing. We must learn to identify the fact that all of our missed shots are not physical failures of our motion, and we must make a serious attempt to build good mental control and good mental direction.

Never allow the mental and physical phases of your golf swing to get ahead or fall behind one another. They must be perfectly synchronized.

Chapter 13

Observation, Awareness, Feel, and Visualization

Awareness is the realization of what is happening or what you are doing. You cannot be aware of anything unless there is good observation. Observing does not mean that you have to see whatever you are observing with your eyes. When riding in a car you can observe speed but you cannot see it. If you are observing speed, you are aware of it.

However, you can be riding in that same car and be completely oblivious to speed because there is no intent to observe it. You may be admiring the scenery, talking to the passengers, reading, or listening to the radio.

So, in the golf swing, players must observe the club's swinging motion as it is in progress, so that they know whether or not the desired motion or corrective procedure is being produced. Since the golf swing cannot be seen by the player making it, it must be observed through the sense of feel, while at the same time visualizing the desired motion or corrective procedure.

Visualizing means that you have in your mind a picture of what you must do. Without proper visualization, you cannot make a good swing.

The word feel does not refer to how the swing feels, because each swing has its own distinctive feel. No two swings feel exactly the same. We human beings cannot be so consistent in our movements and attitude so as to duplicate them exactly.

There is always some degree of variation, and the conditions under which we make the swings also vary. Therefore, the word feel to the golfer should mean that we sense, or are aware of what is taking place. Following are the reasons why our swings or shots can never feel the same. As you can see, there are many.

1. The keenness with which we observe changes from day to day and sometimes within the same practice period or round of golf.

2. We do not focus our observation on the same thing every time.

3. We do not swing the club with exactly the same acceleration every time.

4. We do not hold the club with exactly the same pressure every time we swing it.

5. We do not make our swing exactly the same size every time.

6. The ball, even if placed on the grass or on a tee by hand, isn't always placed exactly the same.

7. Our stance, depending upon where the ball lies, can change dramatically.

8. We use clubs of different lengths. We seldom hold the club for full shots at the same point we hold it when making three-quarter or half shots, even though we swing the club the same way.

9. The length of the grass around the ball can vary greatly. The direction in which it grows varies at different points on the course, and its resistance to the clubhead as the clubhead goes through it changes a great deal.

10. Wind, rain, and temperature change the feel of the swing dramatically.

In spite of these variables, it is possible to (and indeed the golfer must) make the same movement with the club and must feel (sense, be aware) that the correct movement has been made, even though the feel of the movement itself can never be identical to any other one performed. If conditions remained constant in all respects in these 10 points, then and only then could the swings feel similar. Such consistency and lack of variability in conditions will never exist.

To be good golfers, we must work very diligently to develop a keen sense of observation. At first, we may find some difficulty because:

1. The time element—2-1/2 to 3 seconds to make a golf swing.

2. The tremendous speeds generated in such a short time.

3. The mind tends to become concerned with:

    a.   The result of the shot.

    b.   The rough.

    c.   The hazards, whether sand or water.

    d.   The green.

    e.   The lie of the ball.

    f.   The stance.

    g.   Controlling the golf ball.

    h.   The other players in the group.

    i.   The score.

    j.   The wind.

We must train our mind to observe a movement that in a very short time develops speeds as high as 120 miles per hour.

If our mind is occupied with any or all of the items in #3 above, it will be very difficult for us to observe the movement being performed, and we will not know what is being done. If we observe what the different parts of our bodies do, the movement of the club will not be observed.

To observe properly, we must constantly follow the movement mentally through the sense of feel, awareness, and visualization from the moment the club leaves the ball in our backswing until it reaches the end of our swing.

Observation must be positive in relation to what we wish to do. If our concept is clear in our mind, the observation should be relative to the concept, as only in this way will we know whether or not we accomplish what our concept tells us to do.

Negative observation is the type where the player observes the golf swing only with the intent of finding out what is wrong with it. This works hand in hand with the negative mental attitude discussed earlier, which converts into a corrective attitude. Just as a negative mental attitude is a deterrent factor in the person's ability to produce a correct swing, so is negative observation.

Observation, awareness, feel, and visualization should all be developed so they are concerned only with what the player must do.

Chapter 14

Course Management

What is course management? It is the study of the golf course from the tactical point of view and the application of that study to the actual playing of the golf course. It is the basis for the pattern of play for each hole on the course and includes playing conditions.

Playing conditions include the following:

1. Wind

2. Rain

3. Greens

   a. Hard or soft

   b. Grass

      i. Type (important for grain direction)

      ii. Length

   c. Hazards

      i. Water

      ii. Sand

   d. Shape and accessibility

4. Fairways

   a. Soft (watered) or hard

   b. Grass (Length)

   c. Hazards

      i. Water

      ii. Sand

   d. Width

   e. Boundaries

To get the most out of your game, you must consider all of these conditions. Every one changes the playability of every hole.

Perhaps the most bothersome is wind. Wind is present everywhere on the golf course, unlike a lake, stream, or out of bounds that affects a particular hole or shot. Wind affects every hole and every shot, and it affects our par and birdie possibilities. Very seldom is golf played when wind is not an influential element.

Different players are affected by different wind directions in particular ways. Right-handed players who tend to slice their shots are bothered by a left to right wind, those who tend to hook are bothered by a right to left wind, and those with a tendency to hit the ball high are bothered by the wind blowing directly into them.

Wind has a drying effect on greens and makes them unresponsive to backspin, requiring, therefore, a specific type of shot to be played to the green.

Course management and tactical play vary with each player, and this variation is controlled by:

- The distance you send the golf ball.
- The versatility of your game, i.e., your repertoire of different types of shots.
- Condition of ball landing areas.

An Example of Course Management

Let us take a particular hole and study it under varying conditions. The hole is the 15th hole at the Milwaukee Country Club in River Hills, Wisconsin (see diagram). This is a par 5.

Without Wind

This newly designed hole presents certain situations that require good course management. Assuming a quiet day windwise, it is possible to drive over Point B and some players over point C. So from the drive standpoint, it can play straight away. For the second shot on this quiet day, it is possible for the longer hitters to reach the green without too much difficulty.

However, if the flag is at point E, it requires a very good shot to carry the bunker and it must not fade. If it does, the ball could end up in the river. If the flag is at point F, the distance between G and H is very important since at that point, the green is quite shallow. The ball must reach the green high and land softly or it could roll into the bunker behind the green. An alternative shot is to play a shot that allows the ball to land short of the green and roll slowly to the flag.

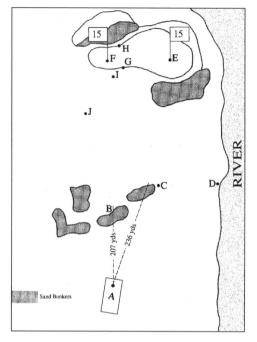

Figure 46

With Wind

If the wind is blowing against you, it will be almost impossible to carry the bunkers, so that if you want to drive on line AB you would reach the bunker with the driver but not carry it. You should use a 3- or 4-wood. If you decide to drive on line AC, there is a dilemma because if you hit a very good drive you also could reach the bunker. You should direct your drive to a point halfway between points C and D. If the hole is on the right side of the green, the hole will then be played as a double dogleg.

Regardless of the location of the ball on the fairway, you should play your second shot in the direction of point F so the ball will end up in the vicinity of point I. From there, it is easy to chip to any part of the green. If the chip does not end up close enough for one putt and a birdie, the worst score you can get is par for the hole.

As I mentioned, wind dries the top layer of the soil, and the shorter the grass, the more severe this is. In this hole, if the wind is a relatively strong factor, and the flagstick is at point F, with a shallow green at that point, your chances of stopping the ball on the green are rather slim. In view of this situation, point I becomes even more important. With a favoring wind, it would be even more difficult to stop the ball on the green.

With this type of analysis, you can come up with a method of play that is "sure" to guarantee a par, and with good chipping a possible birdie. This hole should be played as a double dogleg. From the tee to the right side of the fairway and the second shot to the left side of the fairway. If you do not hit a long ball and your second shot ends at point J, you can still hit your third shot, using the widest view of the green, to any part of it without having to go over any hazard.

Rain and Wet Greens

Rain complicates play in other ways. The most difficult thing, when playing in the rain is keeping your hands, glove, and grips dry. An umbrella is your salvation. Use it to keep your clubs dry and keep a dry towel among the stays. Although this is not directly involved in course management, it can affect the quality of your performance.

The ball has a difficult time flying with directness when the dimples get full of water, producing what are called flyers, which simply means the ball flies out of control. Since you cannot touch the ball, it is impossible to change this condition, except on the green, so this type of flight must be expected.

It helps to play half or three-quarter iron shots, which impart a more direct flight to the ball, and cancel somewhat the smoothness of the ball cover when the dimples are filled with water. Woods produce better shots when more loft is used for fairway shots. When teeing off, do not allow too much time to lapse between the time you place the ball on the tee and the time the club strikes it.

On the green, wipe your ball dry and replace it when you are ready to putt. It is advisable to read the putt without the ball on the green. If you read from the opposite direction of the putt and the marker cannot be seen, the ball has to be on the green, but once the line has been determined, the ball should be dried again. Don't forget to mark it before you pick it up.

Rain can be responsible for mud adhering to the golf ball, which will severely distort the flight of the shot. Again half or three-quarter shots with less lofted clubs will help maintain better control of the flight of the ball.

Putting will be greatly affected by wet greens, so before you putt check your line to see if you have to putt over casual water. Don't forget that the rules allow you to move the ball so that you do not have to putt through water—the new position of your ball, however, must be no nearer the hole.

Wet greens change the selection of clubs when chipping. Do not play long pitch and run shots because the ball will not run. Stay with the lofted clubs and land the ball closer to the hole than you normally would.

Using Common Sense

A very important attitude that leads to good course management, and thus to better scoring, is to face the situation, if in trouble, with coolness and most of all good common sense. If your ball ends up in sand or in the woods, do not play the hole as if the ball were in the middle of the fairway. So many players will, for example, try to play a wood or a long iron out of a bunker with a high bank in front of them. The ball fails to carry the bank, hits into it, rolls back into the bunker or just bounces out rolling a few yards. A better decision would have been to play any club from a 6-iron to a sand iron, depending on how close the ball is to the bank. This club selection would have cleared the bank nicely and given the player a lot more distance.

When the ball ends up in the trees, don't expect it to fly through the branches and leaves—it is most unlikely that it will, the odds are not in your favor. Because of your gamble, you could end up in a much worse position. Accept being in the woods and play any shot that will return the ball to the fairway or to a position that gives you a clear shot to the green, even though you may not be able to reach it.

Summary

- Always play so that the direction of your shot is away from trouble. If there is trouble on both sides of the fairway, take the midpoint between the trouble on the left side and the trouble on the right side and use that point as your target. This way your allowance for error on either side of the target line is greater and safer.

- When teeing off, if there is an out of bounds boundary, water, or sand on the right side of the fairway, tee off from the right side of the tee. If the trouble is on the left side, then tee off from the left side of the tee. By doing this the ball is directed away from the trouble.

- Do not expect to play a particular hole the same way every time you play it. Adjust to conditions and to the way your game feels on that particular day.

Appendixes

15 Ideas Detrimental to Building and Maintaining A Good Golf Swing

1. **Grip tighter with the last 3 fingers of the high hand and very lightly with the fingers of the low hand.**

   a. The pressure used to grip a golf club should be equal from the little finger of the high hand to the thumb and forefinger of the low hand.

   b. The pressure will move up and down the grip in response to the velocity with which the club is being swung.

   c. The greater the velocity, the tighter the last three fingers will hold, but this is entirely a subconscious reaction.

2. **The player should determine how tightly the club should be held.**

   a. The amount of pressure used in the grip (both hands considered) is directly proportional to the length of the club to be used and the velocity that will be generated.

   b. The correct pressure is set subconsciously not consciously.

   c. Whatever pressure the player sets at address should be maintained *constant* throughout the swing.

3. **When swinging the club away from the ball in the backswing, use only the high hand, and allow the low hand to go along for the ride.**

   a. The low hand is a very important factor in a good backswing for:

      i.   Retaining the correct plane.

      ii. Maintaining the clubhead in a square attitude.

      iii. Maintaining necessary club control.

   b. Both hands must be used to the same degree in the backswing so that they do not work against each other.

   c. Lack of use of the low hand in the backswing will result in high hand dominance, which will lay the club off and make the backswing very flat.

4. Keep the left arm straight and left elbow close to your body.

Cannot be done and retain the correct plane. If attempted, backswing will:

a. Become very flat.

b. Be very short.

5. Stay down and keep the head down.

Both destroy the synchronization between the club and the body. Rather than making an effort to stay down or keep the head down, keeping the eye on the ball is what should be emphasized. The ball should be followed once it has been struck with the clubhead. The player should finish in a very erect position and facing the target. Staying down prevents this.

6. Keep the left arm straight.

a. Player will attempt to keep the left arm straight throughout the swing causing the clubhead to be open at impact.

b. Ball will slice and the shot will have no distance.

c. The left arm should be permitted to extend and remain extended without tension so that it can fold after impact. *Everyone's extension potential is different.*

7. Pull with the left hand to start the forward swing from the end of the backswing.

This is bad because:

a. The force applied to pull has a straight line attitude and the swing is circular.

b. Since the swing is circular, everything a player does to produce the golf swing must have a circular attitude.

c. Pulling will tense the target side arm and decrease the freedom in the wrist.

d. Result will be:

i. Shot will be rather short.

ii. Shot will be sliced.

8. **Shift the weight to the back foot in the backswing.**

   a. This causes a loss of the center of the swing.

   b. Produces swaying.

   c. Produces great inconsistency because the center of the swing must be re-established prior to impact or the clubhead will not return square to the target line.

   d. Requires a lot of practice to maintain proper timing and re-establish the swing center.

9. **Shift the weight to the front foot on the forward swing.**

   a. Weight should and does transfer to the front foot in perfect synchronization with the club's swinging motion as a response to that motion.

   b. The player can never establish the proper rate of transfer consciously. It will be done either too fast or too late, mostly it will be too fast. The player will tend to slice.

   c. The weight transfer to the front foot should take place in the same manner as it does when throwing a ball underhand—*naturally* and as a result of the motion.

10. **Keep the weight on the inside of the back foot in the backswing.**

    a. Any effort to do this will restrict the shoulder and hip turn.

    b. Encourages swinging from the outside in the forward swing.

11. **Get the target side hip out of the way on the forward swing.**

    a. Hip action as all other body motions should be a response to the club's swinging motion.

    b. Hips have three types of motions as the swing is performed.

       i.   They tilt.

       ii. They turn.

       iii. They move forward.

   c. In order for a player to do this properly, the following would have to be known.

      i. What percentage of each of 11-b would have to be produced.

      ii. When does each type of motion start.

      iii. At what rate must each be done.

      iv. How much of each must be done for each club used. As the clubs become longer and the planes flatten, the percentage of each in 11-b changes.

12. Hit down with the irons and up with the woods.

   a. A swing is a backward and forward motion—to and fro. It doesn't change because the clubs used have different names.

   b. In the above definition of the swing there is no down and there is no up.

   c. The club should be swung with the intention of sending the ball to the target not with the intention of driving the ball into the ground or up into the sky.

   d. If an object is being propelled in a certain direction with another object, the direction of both objects must be the same.

   e. Only two shots in golf require a downward attitude and both are in sand bunkers.

      i. A buried lie.

      ii. Fried egg or crater-like lie.

13. Use the legs, feet, hips, and shoulders in the forward swing.

   a. The use of any of the above prevents:

      i. Squareness of the clubhead at impact.

      ii. Swinging the club in a forward direction—toward the target.

   b. The body must be allowed to respond naturally to the swinging motion—it should not be used to control it.

   c. Any effort to use any part of the body destroys the swinging motion.

    d. Depending on how different parts of the body are used, the results can be:

        i. Sliced shots.

        ii. Pulled shots.

        iii. Very short shots.

        iv. Never good solid straight shots.

14. Swing the club away from the ball in one piece in the backswing.

    a. Clubhead will tend to get closed.

    b. The club cannot be swung to the end of the backswing in one piece. A one-piece takeaway prevents the wrist action necessary to get the club over the shoulder. The club can only be taken with this idea about half way back, at which point the player must do something additional to complete the backswing.

    c. There is a tendency to tilt the shoulders excessively thereby preventing the necessary shoulder turn.

15. Swing the club straight back from the ball.

    a. This will produce an outside-in swing unless at the beginning of the forward swing, the club is re-routed to return it on the proper plane. It will make the ball go straight left with the short irons and with the longer irons and woods, slicing will be the norm.

    b. Since the swing is circular, nothing involved in producing it can move in a straight line.

    c. Anything other than a circular movement away from the ball will require the player to manipulate the club in an effort to return the club to the ball square to the target line.

Glossary of Terms

ACCELERATION A constant increase of speed per unit of time or space.

ARM The section of the upper extremity from the shoulder to the elbow.

AWARENESS Sensing what you are doing at the time you are doing it.

CENTER

> For the player: The midpoint between the shoulders.

> Of the stance: The point where a perpendicular line from the center for the player meets the ground.

CENTRIFUGAL FORCE The force created when the golf club is swung. It is an outward pull from the center.

CHANGE OF PACE An effort exerted by the player to increase speed as the clubhead reaches the ball.

CLUBFACE CLOSED Clubface faces to the left (right for left handed players) but the loft is decreased.

CLUBFACE OPEN Clubface faces to the right (left for left handed players) but the loft is increased.

CLUBFACE OUT OF SQUARE Clubface faces to the right or left but retains its normal loft.

COIL The result of swinging the club over the shoulder with the hands in the backswing with the wrists extremely free. If wrists are firm, there can be no coil.

CONCENTRATION Sustained thought over a certain period of time.

CONSTANT Something invariable or unchanging.

DIFFERENTIAL RELAXATION Every part of the body, arms, forearms, and wrists remain relaxed, except the fingers that are holding the golf club.

DIRECTION The line or course on which something (golf club) is moving or is intended to move.

FEEL To sense what is being done. Feel cannot be reproduced, it depends on an action that comes first. Feel also refers to sensing distance when less than full shots are used such as in the short game.

FLEXIBILITY Lack of muscle tension.

FOLLOW-THROUGH The name given to that part of the swing from the ball to wherever the swing ends. The follow-through is produced by the speed of the swing, it is not produced by the player.

GRIP PRESSURE Holding the club with sufficient force to control the length of the club and the speed with which you want to swing it. The pressure should be constant from the player's standpoint throughout the golf swing.

HAND ACTION Using the hands to thrust the clubhead as it approaches the ball in order to create more power.

HIT, A A sudden exertion of effort to send the ball on its way.

INTERFERENCE Anything that changes the initial intent of the player after the swing has been started.

LEAVE IT ALONE Once the forward swing has been started, there should be no additions or subtractions. Examples of additions are trying to increase speed as the ball is approached or trying to give the shot great height through swing changes. An example of subtraction is decreasing the swing speed, thinking that too big a swing has been made and the ball is going to go too far.

LEFT-HAND DOMINANCE Using the left hand exclusively in the backswing. It causes the plane to become flatter (more horizontal—laid off.) Both hands should be used equally.

LEVERAGE Action which consists of opposite forces.

LIE How the ball rests on the ground.

LIES, TYPES OF SIDEHILL LIES are those where the hill rises or descends to the right or to the left of the player facing the ball. One foot is always higher than the other.

UPHILL LIES are those where the hill rises in front of the player. The ball is above the player's feet.

DOWNHILL LIES are those where the hill descends in front of the player. The ball is below the player's feet.

MENTAL DIRECTION The mind telling the muscles what to do.

MENTAL DIRECTION, DETERIORATION OF Taking good results for granted. Becoming mentally lax, losing focus on what has to be done, expecting the good results to just happen, as though the player is not involved.

OBSERVATION Being aware of what is going on. Being aware that what should be done is being done. This is positive observation.

PATH The arc described by the clubhead. The path of the forward swing is not the same as the path of the backswing.

PLANE The inclination of the circle the golf club makes when it is swung, with respect to the horizontal level of the ground.

POINT OF MAXIMUM SPEED The point where the club swings the fastest. The acceleration must be maintained to this point, which is the midpoint of the arc.

PRACTICE Just hitting balls is not practice. Practice should be performed with a goal in mind.

RADIUS A line extending from the center to the curve.

RESPONSE The activity of the body resulting from the golf swing.

RHYTHM The relationship of one side of the swing to the other.

SPEED The result of acceleration.

SWING A to and fro motion—backward and forward.

SYNCHRONIZATION The result of synchronizing, which means to make motions exactly simultaneously. To have actions take place at the same time.

TARGET The destination—what we want to reach.

TEMPO The rate or speed of motion.

THOUGHT A mental direction to accomplish or do something specific.

TIMING All parts of the club reach the moment of truth at the same time.

TRAJECTORY, LAWS OF The farther an object is propelled, the higher it is sent. The shorter the distance, the lower it is sent.

TRUTH, MOMENT OF When the clubface meets the golf ball.

VISUALIZATION Forming a mental image of what you are trying to do.

WRIST ACTION The involuntary reaction of the hinges called "wrists" to the uncoiling motion of the golf club.

Helpful Thoughts

- Good mental direction is essential to perform the correct physical motion.

- Believe in the swinging motion and trust it.

- There are no tricks or gimmicks that will produce a correct swing.

- Do not let the lie of the ball control how you will swing.

- Thought is not motion. Thinking of what you want to do is not enough. You must convert the thought into motion.

- Do not keep trying to patch the swing.

- If you do not visualize what you are trying to do, you cannot do it.

- If the ball is resting high on the grass in the rough, do not ground the clubhead—hold it up even with the ball.

- Do not take the swing for granted—always direct it properly with your concept.

- Do not let the clubhead rest behind the ball if you are having difficulty starting the backswing. Start swinging the moment the clubhead touches the grass.

- Negative observations cause you to interfere with your swinging motion.

- Do not try to swing the club faster than you are able to control it.

- Trust and accept the swinging motion when correct, even though it may not feel "good" or "right" to you.

- There should be no conscious hitting action as the clubhead approaches the ball.

- Interference is anything you do that changes your swing once it is in progress.

- Interferences are not always the same as to type and/or degree.

- Do not try *not* to do something. Try to do what is correct.

- Be aware of your tendencies or trends. Check them when you start to hit bad shots.

- Observing your swing while performing it is more important than trying to determine what you did after it is over.

- Observation is knowing what you are doing as you are doing it.

- A swinging attitude requires constant grip pressure.

- Do not get stuck mentally either on the backswing or forward swing—visualize the swing as a whole.

- All clubs should be swung with the same concept, the same purpose, and the same acceleration.

- There should be no effort. Effort is work and work destroys the swinging motion.

- Do not permit the ball flight to control you and therefore the way you attempt to swing.

- Swing the club, speedwise, as you feel on the day you play.

- Do not think of something going wrong with your swing—or it will.

- Lighten the grip slightly if you have a feeling of overpowering the club or if the club feels too light.

- The swinging motion of the club propels the golf ball, *not you.*

- Sudden actions destroy the swing.

- There must be complete freedom—no muscular tension.

- You do not lift the ball into the air. The loft of the club does it.

Historical Information

The Legacy of Ernest Jones

Ernest Jones was a British golf professional. In 1915 while serving in the British Army in France during World War I, he suffered an injury to his right leg which eventually required amputation.

In 1916 he left a British Army hospital missing his right leg. He had been a fine player before the war, enjoyed competition, and had played well enough to qualify several times for the British Open Championship.

At the age of 18 he had become an assistant at the Chislehurst Golf Club so his interest in the golf profession was in his blood from a very young age.

In spite of his disability, he was determined that his playing golf had to remain a part of his life so after leaving the service, he returned to the game he loved, golf. On his first round, played at Royal Norwich he scored 83, a short time later playing at Clacton he scored a 72. Both while swinging on one leg.

This was an astounding accomplishment and launched him into the development of what was to become the Ernest Jones system "Swing the Clubhead." If he could play as he did during his early convalescence without one leg, there had to be a way to teach the game with greater simplicity and common sense.

In 1924 at the invitation of Marion Hollins, the founder of the Women's National Golf and Tennis Club in Long Island, he became the golf instructor at that club. During World War II that club was abandoned and Mr. Jones began teaching indoors at the Spalding Building on Fifth Avenue, in New York City. He found that he preferred to teach indoors because the students could concentrate more effectively on their swing than on where the ball was going.

Through the years he became a very sought after instructor whose students included Betty Hicks, Virginia Van Wie, Elizabeth Ryan, Glenna Collett, Betty Jameson, Phil Farley, George Schniter, Horton Smith, Mary L. Brown, and others. Regardless of the player's status in the game, beginners or championship caliber, the emphasis was always on what was right and not on what was wrong.

Although Mr. Jones' success was well documented and well known, his teaching system was not readily accepted by the teaching profession to the detriment of the students as well as the profession. When my father and I would discuss the Jones concept with our colleagues, the comment "it can't be done that way" was constantly made.

Fortunately, today's teaching golf professional is very different. The PGA of America has been instrumental through its educational programs in opening up the minds of today's teachers of golf. Those of us who so strongly believe in the Jones principle have the opportunity to present those ideas to more and more teachers. The present day golf instructor is willing to listen and discuss new ideas even though they may be very new to them. Mr. Jones would be avidly listened to today.

Mr. Jones' stature in the golf teaching profession of today has been so highly regarded that he was introduced into the World Golf Teachers Hall of Fame in 1977 at the inaugural induction ceremony. Mr. Jones passed away in 1965 at the age of 77.

The de la Torre Family

My father, Angel de la Torre, became the golf professional at the Real Club de la Puerta de Hierro on the outskirts of Madrid in 1918. At this course, which was the Royal golf course, he became the golf instructor to the king of Spain as well as to the other members of the Royal family. He had won the Spanish Open Championship in 1916 and 1917. There was no Open in 1918, and in 1919 he won it again. In 1920 he set a course record with a 65, which was 12 below par on this Madrid course, which was considered one of the most interesting and difficult outside of England. He was 23 years old. He was to again win the Spanish Open Championship in 1923, 1925 and 1935.

My parents were married that year after Dad's first visit to England to play in the British tournaments. (It was during that visit that my father and Ernest Jones met.) The professional was given living quarters at the club, and I was born on October 6, 1921 in the apartment provided above the golf shop at the Royal golf course in Madrid.

My father soon made some small wooden golf clubs for me, which I still have, and probably as soon as I could walk he began to teach me to swing

Published in British golf magazines in 1922—14 months old

First trophy, 1938, at 17 yrs.

From an article published in Madrid, 1923

3½ years old

7 years old

Milwaukee Country Club—2000

225

and hit balls. He told me that he would line up a row of balls and I would proceed up the line hitting one ball after another. Since Dad had become a popular figure in Spain, my "exploits" came to the attention of the members of the club and the press and soon photographs of me hitting golf balls appeared not only in the local Madrid press but in U.S. and English golf magazines. In one magazine clipping that my parents saved I am pictured and credited as being the world's youngest golfer at the age of 14 months.

No one taught my father to play golf. He came from an extremely poor family. His uncle, Pedro de la Torre, was the "greenskeeper" in what was actually land belonging to the King. That land became the Club de las Cuarenta Fanegas and it was the first golf course in Spain. Dad caddied there full time beginning as a very young 7 or 8 year old boy. Subsequently more of the Royal lands in the outskirts of Madrid were ceded and the Puerta de Hierro golf course was built. Dad then caddied there also full time, accompanying his father, Ricardo de la Torre y Torres, who worked on the grounds.

Dad must have been a keen observer even then and learned by himself just watching those for whom he caddied. He learned the principles and how to apply them all by himself. At age 13 he won the caddie tournament at the Royal club and a few years later he became its professional. We are not aware that he had any formal schooling at all since the family's poverty forced him to work since early in his boyhood. Yet, just as he did with golf, he taught himself good Spanish, French, and later English and was able to teach in all three languages.

The fact that he himself had learned to play as a young boy, I am sure contributed to his immediately starting me on the same path. I too learned good Spanish, French, and English, and the early direction I was given may well have made my success in golf possible.

In spite of having to leave Spain because of the Spanish Civil War, Dad was never without a job. Shortly after the de la Torre family was reunited in October 1936, through the efforts of Ernest Jones, his services as a golf instructor were secured by Bill Hickey, who was the golf professional at the Brookside Municipal Golf Course in Pasadena, California. This is the golf course next to the Rose Bowl.

226

By chance, there was another golf professional who was visiting Bill Hickey at that time, and he needed an assistant at the Lake Shore Country Club in Glencoe, Illinois, where he was the head golf professional. This professional's name was Eddie Loos and he took Dad to Lake Shore as his assistant.

Lake Shore Country Club retired Dad in 1967 after 30 years of dedicated service. One of the members of the club was very influential at the Tamarisk Country Club in Palm Springs, California and arranged for Dad to teach during the winter months at Tamarisk, which he did for many winters. During his first winter of retirement he called me one day with great excitement in his voice and he said "I have a new job." The person in charge of the golf course at the Glenview Naval Air Station in Glenview, Illinois had heard of his retirement and told him that they would love to have him teach there. Dad didn't have to think twice to accept. So he would teach at Glenview in the summers and at Tamarisk in the winters.

Dad taught until April 1983, and at the age of 86 he passed away that August. At that time he and I had been in the golf business for 107 years.

Manuel de la Torre

Born in Madrid, Spain on October 6, 1921

Father: Angel de la Torre, who was the first Spanish golf professional. His first position was the Real Club de la Puerta de Hierro. I was born in my parents' apartment located above the Golf Shop at this club. Left Spain to join my father in the United States during the Spanish Civil War and arrived in this country in October 1936.

Attended Highland Park High School, Highland Park, Illinois.

Captained the golf team at Highland Park High School, 1939–1940

Lake County High School Champion, 1940

1940 Attended Northwestern University and graduated in 1947 with a degree in Business Administration.

Northwestern University Freshman Golf Champion, 1942

Runner Up—National Intercollegiate Championship, 1942

Playing Record and Awards

Finished 3rd in Tucson Open—after leading for 3-1/2 rounds, 1950
  Finished 2nd to Cary Middlecoff in Lakewood Open, Long Beach, California, 1951

Named Head Golf Professional at the Milwaukee Country Club, 1951
  Prior to this assignment, I was my Father's assistant for three years at the Lake Shore Country Club in Glencoe, Illinois (1948–1950)

Wisconsin State Open Champion, 1952, 1953, 1955, 1961, 1968

Wisconsin State PGA Medal Play Champion, 1953, 1955, 1957, 1959, 1970

Wisconsin Golfer of the Year, 1953

Winner Capital Times Invitational—Madison, Wisconsin, 1954

Course Record—64 (36/28=64) at South Hills C. C., Fond du Lac, Wisconsin during the PGA Medal Play Championship, 1955

Wisconsin Golf Professional of the Year, 1955, 1956, 1965, 1969

Shot 29 on the last 9 holes of the last 18 holes of the Tucson Open, 1957

Course Record—64 at Milwaukee Country Club, 1957

First round leader—65 at Miller Open, Milwaukee, Wisconsin, 1957

Course Record—67 at Currie Park Golf Club, Milwaukee, Wisconsin, 1958

National Vice President PGA District #6, 1959, 1960, 1961

Course Record—67 at Berwind C. C., Puerto Rico, 1960

Led Milwaukee Open after third round, 1960

Course Record—65 at Monroe Country Club, Monroe, Wisconsin, 1961

Tied for 17th in National PGA Championship—Dallas, Texas, 1963

Cherryland Open Champion, Wisconsin, 1963, 1964

Course Record—65 at Peninsula State Park Golf Course, Wisconsin, 1964

Winner, Hope of Tomorrow Championship—Palm Springs, California, 1965

Course Record on second 9 holes—30 at Indian Bend C. C. Scottsdale, Arizona during Club Professional Championship, 1968

Westview Invitational Champion, Marshfield, Wisconsin, 1972

Wisconsin State PGA Senior Champion, 1972, 1974, 1976, 1987

National Open Seniors Classic Champion, 1973

Inducted into the Wisconsin Golf Hall of Fame, 1975

Winner Calderwood Open (36/33 = 66) Fond du Lac, Wisconsin, 1975

3rd Place National PGA Senior Championship, Disneyworld, 1976

Wisconsin State PGA Match Play Champion, 1976

2nd Wisconsin State PGA Medal Play Championship, 1976

3rd Wisconsin State Open Championship, 1976

Received Wisconsin Section Horton Smith Award, 1977, 1982, 1994

Tied for 1st Place in National PGA Senior Championship, Disneyworld—
   Lost in the playoff, 1978

Tied for 3rd Place in Wisconsin State Open Championship, 1980

Received the 1st National PGA Teacher of the Year Award, 1986

Named by *Golf Magazine* in the Top Fifty Best Teachers in America, 1991

Named by *Golf Magazine* in the Top 100 Best Teachers in America, 1995,
   1999, 2000, 2001

Wisconsin PGA Teacher of the Year, 1996

Was retired as Head Professional by Milwaukee Country Club, 1996

Was retained as Golf Instructor by Milwaukee Country Club, 1997

Inducted into Northwestern University's Hall of Fame, February 11, 2000

Ranked 20th "Best Instructors in America" by Golf Digest, 2000

Ranked 1st "Best Instructors in Wisconsin" by Golf Digest, 2000

Wisconsin PGA Involvement

Secretary–Treasurer, 3 years

President, 3 years

Chairman of Section Tournament Committee, 3 years

Chairman of Major Sites Selection Committee, 15 years

Have served the Wisconsin Section in one capacity or another every year
   since 1952.

Sectional Educational and Clinic Programs

Illinois Section (Program was for Assistants)

Iowa Section

New York Section, 1982

Georgia Section, 1982

Wisconsin Section, 1985

Colorado Section, 1991

Carolinas Section (Winter Educational Seminar), 1991

Wisconsin Section (Spring Educational Seminar), 1991

Southern California Section (Educational Seminar), 1993

Rocky Mountain Section (Educational Seminar), 1993

Pacific Northwest Section (Educational Seminar), 1993

Northern California Section, Nevada Chapter (Educational Seminar), 1994

Gateway Section (Educational Seminar), 1994

Indiana Section (Educational Seminar), 1994

Wisconsin Section (Assistants' Educational Seminar), 1994

National Golf Foundation Teaching Seminars

Pheasant Run, Illinois, 1976

Dayton, Ohio, 1977

Kansas City, Missouri, 1978

San Diego, California, 1986

National PGA Involvement

Delegate to Annual Meeting , 6 years

Vice President for District #6 for 3 years, 1959, 1960, 1961 Chairman of the Manufacturers Relations Committee, 1959, 1960, 1961 Speaker at the First PGA Coaching and Teaching Summit, 1988

Speaker at the Second PGA Coaching and Teaching Summit, 1990

Speaker at the Third PGA Coaching and Teaching Summit, 1992

Teaching Workshops

1978	Scottsdale, Arizona	with Al Mengert
1979	Disneyworld, Florida	with Gary Wiren
1981	Houston, Texas	with Paul Runyan
1982	Seabrook Island, S.C.	with Dick Farley
1983	Atlanta, Georgia	with John Gerring
1983	Seattle, Washington	with John Gerring
1984	Indianapolis, Indiana	with Carl Lohren
1985	Charlotte, N.C.	with Kent Kayce
1986	Dallas, Texas	with Jim Suttie
1986	Atlanta, Georgia	with David Leadbetter
1987	Palm Springs, Cal.	with Bill Strausbaugh
1987	Sacramento, Cal.	with Graig Shankland and Dr. Dick Coop
1987	Baton Rouge, La.	with Guy Wimberly
1988	Scottsdale, Arizona	with Jim Flick and Dr. David Cook
1988	Tulsa, Oklahoma	with Conrad Rehling
1989	PGA National	with Bill Strausbaugh and Dr. Bob Rotella
1989	Louisville, Kentucky	with Conrad Rehling and Mike Hebron
1990	PGA National	with Conrad Rehling and Chuck Cook
1991	Spokane, Washington	with Conrad Rehling
1992	PGA National	with Conrad Rehling
1993	Oklahoma City, OK	with Bill Davis
1994	Palm Springs, Cal.	with William J. Madonna
1995	Woodlands, Texas	with William J. Madonna
1996	PGA National	with Mike McTeigue
1997	Las Vegas, Nevada	during International Golf Show

Resident Schools

1983	Louisville, Kentucky	for Bobby Vaughn
1984	Mt. Clemens, Michigan	for Tom Piper

Foreign Educational Involvement

Conducted bilingual (English and Spanish) clinics at all stops of the Caribbean Tour during the 15 years I was Caribbean Tour Assistant Director.

Conducted a two-day seminar at the Dorado Beach Hotel, Puerto Rico for the Puerto Rican PGA, which is a Chapter of the Florida PGA. 1977

Subjects Presented

1. Merchandising and Golf Shop Operations.
2. Inventory Control.
3. Simple Bookkeeping for the Golf Shop.
4. Public relations with relation to Club Manager and Superintendent.
5. Conducting golf lessons.
6. Clinic and demonstration of teaching concept.
7. Individual instruction for the professionals.

First day's session was conducted in Spanish, and second in English

Conducted a seven-day Seminar for the Colombian Golf Professionals at the invitation of the Colombian Golf Federation. The purpose of the Seminar was to improve the teaching of the Colombian professionals. Seminar was conducted in Spanish, and was held in Bogota, Colombia, 1977

Conducted a seven-day Seminar for the Venezuelan PGA in Caracas, Venezuela, 1982

Returned to Caracas for two weeks of clinics and Teaching Seminar 1983 During these two weeks, the following was presented:

Clinics and individual member instruction at three different clubs in the city.

Conducted three clinics for the Venezuelan Golf Federation during the Venezuelan Amateur Championship held during the last three days of my stay in Caracas.

Conducted two days of clinics and teaching demonstrations for the Venezuelan PGA

All work was conducted in Spanish.

Spoke at the First Canadian Coaching and Teaching Summit, 1989

Miscellaneous Activities

I have been involved in teaching LPGA Tour Players since 1961:

Carol Mann, 15 years

Pam Higgins

Pam Barnett

Mary Lou Crocker

Sherri Steinhauer, 12 years

Martha Nause, 22 years

Have been involved in teaching players from the Senior Men's Tour:

Bobby Brue

Tommy Aaron

LPGA Teaching Seminar—St. Petersburg, Florida, 1985

Public Clinic and Demonstration—Mangrove Municipal Golf Course in St. Petersburg, Florida, 1985

Two-day schools for Gary Sowinski at River Plantation G. C., Conroe, Texas, 1984, 1986, 1987, 1988

Golf Schools (de la Torre, Brue, Mattioli Golf Schools) - Pewaukee, Wisconsin 1984, 1986, 1987

Instructed in a two-day Golf School—Dallas Texas—Hosted By Mary Lou Crocker, LPGA member, 1998

Seminars to Teach the de la Torre System of Teaching

Two-day Seminar	Moon Valley C. C. Phoenix, Arizona	1993
Two-day Seminar	Moon Valley C. C. Phoenix, Arizona	1995
Three-day Seminar	Moon Valley C. C. Phoenix, Arizona	1997
Three-day Seminar	Moon Valley C. C. Phoenix, Arizona	1998
Three-day Seminar	Moon Valley C. C. Phoenix, Arizona	1999
Three-day Seminar	Moon Valley C. C. Phoenix, Arizona	2000

Leaving Wartime Spain

When I attended Highland Park High School in Highland Park, Illinois, I was asked to write an essay about my family's experience when we left Spain in 1936 to come to the United States. I have copied this essay and it is exactly as I wrote it in 1939, three years after arriving in the United States.

"Leaving your native country is an experience which you do not forget very soon.

Sometimes because you are leaving for the first time, the excitement of your being in a country entirely different from your own makes such an impression upon your mind that you will always recall that experience. Sometimes, as is my case, you leave because the country has been driven into a devastating war.

The Spanish Civil War started in July, 1936. As my father had gone to foreign countries to play in different golf tournaments, we found ourselves—my mother, my brother and I—in the center of Spain, Madrid, the scene of many experiences which I had never thought of having.

My father left in May, 1936, and by July of the same year he was in the United States. He hadn't been in this country since 1934, and if he had decided not to come in 1936, all of us would have had to remain in Spain. Our correspondence with him was very limited because every letter going into or out of the country was censored, therefore, we could not explain to him how things really stood. But ever since my father had learned of the situation in our country, he had been arranging everything that would facilitate our coming to the United States, so one day after waiting impatiently for a few weeks, we received a document from the consul of Spain in the United States authorizing my father to bring us over here.

Immediately we started inquiring. We went to the American consul who told us that if things couldn't be arranged very soon, we should have to remain in Spain because either the American consulate or the French frontier would be closed very soon.

Before we could get our passport we had to have a special permit from the chief of police, proving that we were free to leave the Spanish territory. It took us about two weeks to get that permit, but we succeeded in getting it. The document my father had sent us was, of course, signed by the Spanish consul in this country, but this paper was worthless unless the signature was identified by the Spanish authorities. Once this was done, we had two things with which to work, so we went to the consulate, and in a few days we had our passport.

For a trip such as the one we were planning we needed quite a bit of money and this was one of the greatest difficulties we had to face. We were allowed three thousand pesetas, one thousand per person, which was all the money one person was allowed to take out of the country. Three thousand pesetas was the equivalent of two hundred dollars, a very small amount for such a long trip and for three persons.

After many worries and after having walked all over Madrid, we had everything arranged by the first of October, and expected to leave the city on the ninth of the month. The first nine days of October were days of much excitement at home, everyone was busy and we had little rest. As our house had been confiscated by the militiamen, nothing could be taken out of the house without their permission, so again we had to get another permit on which our leaving really depended. Militiamen came to search our house to see if they could find anything suspicious, but on their finding nothing, we obtained what we were after—our permit.

October nine soon arrived, it was a bright sunny day like many I had seen before. It seemed as though Madrid were saying good-bye to us and trying to smile in spite of its worries and misfortunes. Saying good-bye to our relatives was one of the hardest things I have ever done, for it was as if we were never to see them again, and yet, who knew? They were left in great danger, and we realized only too well how truly grave the danger was.

There was only one way to leave Spain, through France, and there was only one way out of Madrid, which was from Madrid to Valencia, from Valencia to Barcelona and from there through Port Bou and Cerbere into France. We were to go aboard the ship at Le Havre, and we left Madrid five days before our sailing date which was October 14, Tuesday.

On the train we were among militiamen going to the Valencia fronts to fight. Everything went very well until we arrived at Barcelona, October 10.

It was Friday night. Our passport and every document we had were inspected many times and every time we were told that everything was in
perfect order. At Barcelona, we arrived around eleven o'clock at night.
Everything was dark, there were no lights anywhere, no people were on
the street, it looked like a deserted city. Sleepy and tired as we were, we
found our way to a hotel where we spent the night.

Early Saturday morning, we took the eight o'clock train for Port Bou,
the Spanish side of the border. If we could pass the border without inter-
ruption, our hardest problem would be solved, and since everything was
in such good order, we thought it would be very easy.

We arrived at Port Bou at about ten o'clock, and our baggage was inspected. This inspection decidedly made us lose our temper, everything
was opened and upset, so when they finished, with our patience coming to
an end we practically had to make our luggage all over again. We brought
two big cases of books, and in one we had the Encyclopedia Brittanica.
They took every book out of the case, they looked through them page by
page, and they soon got to the Encyclopedia which to our surprise, they
looked through every volume, twenty eight in number, page by page.
Finally, everything was inspected and we were ready for the last inspection
of our passport, but we did not know that in the very room where this inspection took place we would receive the worst news anyone in our situation could receive.

We were just about to go aboard the French train, when we were called
back and told that we could not continue our trip because there were five
stamps missing in our passport. We went back to the office and presented
an argument which did absolutely nothing for us. We told the agents that
all the way from Madrid we had been told that all our documents were in
perfect order, to which they answered that every stamp we already had on
our passport permitted us to travel to Barcelona, but there we had to get
five more stamps authorizing us to cross the border. There was nothing we
could do but return to Barcelona Saturday afternoon arriving there at five
o'clock, the immigration offices, of course, being closed.

In Port Bou we met an old lady and her son who were going to Cuba,
and they had also been forced back, but were worse off than we were, for

because her son was twenty-one years old they had to remain in Spain. When we heard about this, we felt as though the same thing would happen to us.

Sunday, all offices were closed and we were still on Spanish territory two days before the boat would sail. We were so worried that we didn't know what to do nor where to go. If we should miss the boat, we would lose the tickets for the boat, the tickets from Barcelona to Le Havre, and we would find ourselves without any money to return to Madrid. We had money to remain in Barcelona no more than a few days, but we didn't lose our hope.

At 6:30 Monday morning we were in a long line of people who were there to get their stamps also. We handed our passport in, and waited from six thirty to two o'clock in that terrible building, with no place to sit down and our hope and patience flying back and forth as birds in space. At two o'clock, though not a bit hungry, we had some lunch and when we returned at two thirty, we received the passport with the first two stamps on it. We were then told to go to another immigration office where the last three stamps would be put on in a few minutes, and we would be able to take an afternoon train for Paris. We got to this second office around three in the afternoon only to find it was closed. We waited for a very long time, and before we knew it, it was nine-thirty. Without any place to go, we decided to remain in the building until we would either be chased out or until tired of having us around, the officials would stamp our passport. Luckily it happened just that way, my Mother was ordered into a room where the officers were, and when she came out, I saw on her face the first smile I had seen since we left Madrid for with all our worries she had had no time to laugh nor to smile. At last our passport had been signed.

The time the ship would sail was eleven o'clock on Tuesday morning. It was Monday night and we had to cross France from one end to the other. That night we spent on the train and although it was very hard to sleep on those trains and this was our fourth night on the train, we were so tired that as soon as we sat down we were fast asleep.

The next morning at about seven we woke up, looked out of the window and saw a beautiful day on French soil. We arrived at the Quai

D'Orsay station, the main station in Paris, at ten thirty, half an hour before the boat sailed. In half an hour we had to arrange the taking of our luggage to the ship, we had to go to the Compagnie Transatlantique Francaise, for we sailed on the *Lafayette*, a French ship, so that the company would take charge of the luggage. The French I spoke was a "pot-pourri," one word in Spanish, another in French, and another in English, but I made myself understood and that was all that mattered.

At the company's office we were told that if we left our luggage behind, we could reach the ship in time, and since that was all we were interested in, we decided to have the Company take charge of the luggage and have them send it on the next ship. Unfortunately, the trunk we should have taken with us in the ship we left behind also, so we were left only with the clothes we were wearing. At ten forty-five we reached *La Gare St. Lazare*, the station for Le Havre, where we took the last train ride of our trip, and in ten minutes we were at the harbor.

An incident happened to us at the Le Havre station which I shall never forget. Anxious as we were to go aboard the ship, as soon as we arrived at the station we were left standing alone on the platform with our hand baggage, because I could get no one to carry it. I strained my throat calling for a "porter," but everyone ignored me. Among us three, however, we managed to carry the baggage to the French officials who were to inspect it for the last time. This inspection took only a few minutes, and very soon, after all our hardships. we found ourselves walking on the deck of the *Lafayette* ready to sail for America."

More praise for *Understanding the Golf Swing*

When I began working with Manuel 12 years ago it was as if I had found a treasure. When you read this book you will learn the basic truths and 'feels' of the golf swing through simple thoughts and responses.
—Sherri Steinhauer, golf professional, LPGA

Manuel de la Torre's book, Understanding the Golf Swing, is based on his experience as an outstanding player and generous teacher. I have benefitted from Manuel's guidance, and strongly recommend his philosophy of golf instruction to everyone with an interest in playing the game.
—Bob Brue, golf professional, Senior Tour

By studying, understanding, and applying the concepts Manuel teaches, I competed successfully on the LPGA tour for 22 years. His passion and common sense knowledge of all phases of the game are evident in his teaching and in this book. I feel extremely fortunate to have been a student of Manuel's for the past 23 years, and I know I will use this book over and over again in the years to come. Everyone, amateur or professional, will benefit from it.
—Martha E. Nause, golf professional, LPGA

for additional copies of

Understanding the Golf Swing

Write:

Warde Publishers, Inc.
3000 Alpine Road
Portola Valley, CA 94028

Toll-free order line: (800) 699–2733

ORDER FORM

Please send me _____ copy(ies) of **Understanding the Golf Swing** by Manuel de la Torre at $27.95. (Add $4.50 for first copy and $.50 for each additional copy for packing and shipping. California residents, add $2.24 sales tax per book ordered.) Make check payable to Warde Publishers, Inc.

Total Enclosed = $ _____

Name _____

Organization _____

Address _____

City _____ State _____ Zip _____